# A Practical Guide to Pre-school Inclusion

Chris Dukes and Maggie Smith

Illustrations by Simon Smith

Los Angeles | London | New Delhi
Singapore | Washington DC

First published 2006 | Reprinted 2009

SAGE Publications Ltd
1 Oliver's Yard
55 City Road
London EC1Y 1SP

SAGE Publications Inc.
2455 Teller Road
Thousand Oaks, California 91320

SAGE Publications India Pvt Ltd
B 1/I 1 Mohan Cooperative Industrial Area
Mathura Road
New Delhi 110 044

SAGE Publications Asia-Pacific Pte Ltd
33 Pekin Street #02-01
Far East Square
Singapore 048763

Library of Congress Control Number: 2006928163

A catalogue record for this book is available from the British Library

ISBN-10: 1-4129-2934-2   ISBN-13: 978-1-4129-2934-9
ISBN-10: 1-4129-2935-0   ISBN-13: 978-1-4129-2935-6 (pbk)

Typeset by Pantek Arts Ltd, Maidstone, Kent
Printed and bound in India by Replika Press Pvt. Ltd.
Printed on paper from sustainable resources

A Practical Guide to Pre-school Inclusion

About the authors

Chris Dukes is a qualified teacher with over 20 years experience. She has worked in various London Primary schools as a class teacher and later as a member of the Senior Management Team. Chris has a Masters degree in Special Needs and through her later role as a SENCO and support teacher, many years experience of working with children with a variety of needs. Chris has worked closely with staff teams, mentoring, advising and supervising work with children with additional needs, as well as with other education and health professionals. Chris currently works as an Area SENCO supporting Special Needs Co-ordinators and managers in a wide range of pre-school settings. As well as advising she writes courses, delivers training and produces publications.

Maggie Smith began her career as a Nursery Teacher in Birmingham. She has worked as a Peripatetic teacher for an under 5s EAL Team and went on to become the Foundation Stage manager of an Early Years Unit in Inner London. Maggie helped to set up an innovative unit for young children with behavioural difficulties and has also worked supporting families of children with special needs. Maggie has taught on Early Years BTEC and CACHE courses at a college of Higher Education. Maggie currently works as an Area SENCO supporting Special Needs Co-ordinators and managers in a wide range of pre-scool settings. As well as advising she also writes courses, delivers training and produces publications.

Contents

Acknowledgements

Thanks to our families, especially Jesse, Tom, Nina, Libby and Norman for their support and patience during the writing of this book. Thanks to Stephen Muller for his creative ideas and input. Thanks also to everybody who has supported us in this exciting new adventure.

Introduction

Overheard in the supermarket queue

Mother 1: *How's Tom?*

Mother 2: *Oh, he's fine; he'll be starting nursery soon. He's really looking forward to it – he asks me every day when he is going to start.*

Mother 1: *Which nursery is he going to?*

Mother 2: *He's going to Perfect Children – it's just around the corner from where we live. Your Libby should be starting soon; where's she going to go?*

Mother 1: *We haven't managed to find a place for her to go yet; all the local nurseries either say they're full or that they can't cope with her because of her condition. She's still in nappies and needs help with getting around.*

Mother 2: *I can't believe that! Surely it's against the law for them to say that? Nowadays there is a lot of help and support available; haven't you heard the adverts on the radio about discrimination and the disabled? Nurseries aren't allowed to just turn children away. Especially your Libby – she's lovely. Have you tried Perfect Children?*

Mother 1: *Yes I did go and have a look around but they didn't seem very keen to take her. I think it's because they would have had to make a few adjustments to the room. Anyway, I want her to go somewhere where she will be appreciated and I'll feel comfortable about leaving her. To be truthful I'm really upset about it.*

Mother 2: *I'm really surprised about Perfect Children's attitude and I feel a bit disappointed. Tom and Libby have known each other since they were babies. I think I may have to reconsider where Tom goes you know.*

This is the sort of conversation that we hope would never happen. Sometimes, however, it does for many different reasons, the most common being that practitioners do not feel confident enough about meeting the needs of *all* children.

A Practical Guide to Pre-School Inclusion sets out to allay some of the fears that surround working with children with additional needs. The straightforward step-by-step practical

guide will demystify what is meant by inclusion. In our experience pre-school practitioners always want to do the best for the children in their care.

By working your way through the book or by using the stand-alone chapters you will:

▶ Understand the benefits of inclusion

▶ Be aware of your legal responsibilities

▶ Create inclusive policies

▶ Develop inclusive play

▶ Develop an inclusive environment

▶ Plan for individuals with additional needs

Pre-school practitioners

Each chapter will encourage you to reflect on your setting and identify and plan for improvement. You will be supported by examples of policies, formats to use for taking stock, and ideas for recording information. These can be used as presented in the book or adapted and personalised to suit your setting. The end-of-chapter activities will provide starting points for team discussion.

Tutors and students

Through reading this book you will increase your awareness of the issues surrounding inclusion; you will begin to understand the legislation and develop your own current and future practice. The end-of-chapter activities can be used as short assignments.

Advisers

Use this book to support pre-schools to become more inclusive. Stand-alone chapters can be used as the basis of training or as an audit and planning tool.
The end-of-chapter activities will provide discussion points for staff teams.

A note on the text

The case studies included in this publication are a composite of numerous children in various settings, compiled over the authors' many years of experience, and are not specific to any one child, practitioner or setting.

Throughout this book you will see this CD icon used 💿 this tells you that there is an electronic version of the material you are looking at available on the CD Rom that accompanies the book.

 Inclusion: what it is and why it's good news for everyone

The aim of this chapter is to increase your knowledge of how to develop an inclusive setting. It gives an opportunity to assess how inclusive you currently are. It outlines the benefits of inclusion for your setting and business, as well as explaining the benefits of inclusive practices for parents, children and practitioners. Students, tutors and advisers will find this chapter a good starting point for discussing issues of inclusion.

The chapter sets out:

▶ How being inclusive is good news for your business, parents, children and practitioners

▶ 20 ways to recognise an inclusive setting

▶ A starter quiz – How inclusive is you Pre-school?

It also offers suggestions for additional activities designed to build on the topics covered in the chapter, and a list of recommended further reading.

Being inclusive is good news for your setting

Increasingly, society is becoming more diverse and our Pre-school settings are beginning to reflect this.

Children with additional needs are present throughout all layers of our society. Some of those needs may be short term and others may be lifelong conditions.

Parents and Pre-schools

Working parents and those who want some form of Pre-school education and care for their children are increasingly faced with many choices when it comes to choosing childcare. Some opt for home care using family members, au pairs, nannies or childminders while the increasing majority are choosing from all kinds of Pre-school provision.

The market is competitive and parents are always looking for the very best care for their child.

Some factors parents consider when choosing a Pre-school are:

▶ Can they be sure the well-being of their child is central to the ethos of the setting?

▶ Are the relationships within the setting good?

▶ Does the setting have caring adults?

▶ Is the setting well regarded within the community?

▶ Are any children excluded or disadvantaged within the setting?

▶ Will their child have a rich and stimulating experience based upon his/her individual needs?

▶ Will there be a special person in the setting that their child can depend upon?

A good reputation is usually well earned and always deserved. An inclusive setting is able to offer all of the points outlined above. It follows, then, that an inclusive setting will rank high in popularity as parents see that all children are valued and cared for.

Parents in an inclusive setting can be confident that their child will be valued and will receive the highest possible care.

Ofsted and the Sessional and Full Day Care National Standards

All Pre-school settings need Ofsted (Office for Standards in Education) registration. There is currently a cycle of inspections in place, the outcomes of which are important to all practitioners. While some see the inspection as an opportunity to display their good practice others view an inspection as something to be survived.

Whatever your viewpoint in regard to Ofsted, being well prepared and organised for your inspection is a must.

Ofsted inspectors will refer to 'Outcomes from *Every Child Matters*' (DfES, 2004) together with the '*National Day Care/Sessional Standards*' (DfES, 2001).

Outlined below are some of the factors that may be considered by inspectors when visiting Pre-schools in relation to inclusion and provision for those children with a special educational need.

Standard 10 of the National Standards covers the main area of Special Educational Needs. It states:

> *The registered person is aware that some children may have special needs and is proactive in ensuring the appropriate action can be taken when such a child is identified or admitted to the provision. Steps are taken to promote the welfare and development of the child within the setting in partnership with the parents and other relevant parties.* (DfES, 2003, p. 5)

Pre-school settings are also judged against the five outcomes from *Every Child Matters*. While *Outcome 3* (Enjoy and achieve) and *Outcome 4* (Making a positive contribution) cover issues of inclusion more specifically, all outcomes can be considered relevant.

To satisfy themselves that provision for children with special educational needs is being met, inspectors may address the following issues during their visit:

◗ Children's records

◗ Your written statements about special needs

◗ Your arrangements for caring for children with special needs

◗ How you share information about your provision for children with special needs with parents

Throughout this book you will find advice that will help you work towards becoming a fully inclusive setting.

Chapters 2 and 5 particularly support practitioners as they prepare for their inspections. Examples of the following can be found both in the chapters and on the CD-ROM that accompanies this book:

◗ Planning for individuals' needs using the proformas provided

◗ Sample policies available for direct use or adaptation

◗ Information and suggestions on communicating with parents

Everyone benefits from inclusion

Being an inclusive setting enhances the reputation of any Pre-school. Inclusive settings are usually a commercial success due to their popularity with parents. These settings can also expect their efforts to be recognised by Ofsted.

Here is a summary of the benefits of being inclusive for parents, children and practitioners.

Parents

▶ Feel less isolated as they become part of the wider community

▶ Begin to see that all children are valued and appreciated

▶ Develop strong bonds with nursery staff as mutual respect is developed

▶ Gain a wider view of a diverse society

▶ Develop understanding and empathy with other parents

▶ Learn techniques and skills from practitioners

▶ Are given reassurance that society values their children

Children

▶ Learn that all individuals are different and unique – including themselves

▶ All experience the same opportunities and experiences

▶ All benefit from a broad and balanced, enriched curriculum

▶ Feel they belong and are part of the community

▶ Develop tolerance and empathy as individuals

▶ Experience a growth in self-esteem and social skills

▶ Experience social integration and equality

▶ Learn to be confident and reach for goals

▶ Have all of their needs met

▶ Benefit from extra staffing and the involvement of outside professionals

Practitioners

▶ Benefit from additional training provided by local authority staff and staff from voluntary agencies

▶ Become able to cater for a range of different needs

▶ Gain confidence in their practice and expertise

▶ Learn how to liaise and communicate with outside professionals, e.g. speech therapists or peripatetic teachers

▶ Work together as a team, supporting and learning from each other

▶ Develop close links with parents/carers

▶ Gain greater satisfaction from their chosen profession

Note for employers

Good staff are hard to find and employers need to be able to offer jobs that stretch individuals and offer job satisfaction. An inclusive setting provides much satisfaction and challenge for practitioners.

 Hands-on activity

Role-play or discuss the following scenario:

During a staff meeting a member of the team says, 'I don't know what all this fuss is about. I don't see why we should have to accommodate all types of children here – it's just too much trouble.'

On the following pages you will find useful criteria to help you recognise some of the features of an inclusive setting. In order to help you see how your own setting measures up to these we have included a quiz. This can be done either individually or as a staff team. This will help you to begin to consider the wider issues of inclusion.

20 ways to recognise an inclusive setting

1. The setting is used by a wide cross-section of the local community

2. The staff are flexible and responsive and team work is evident

3. The environment has been carefully considered in terms of accessibility

4. Practitioners have time to reflect and discuss their practice

5. Strong links exist between the setting and community

6. Good use is made of LEA and heath service professionals

7. Staff attend outside training and have regular in-house training sessions

8. A key worker system is being used

9. The setting Special Educational Needs Co-ordinator (SENCO) has time and resources to carry out their duties effectively

10. Pictures and displays represent a diverse society

11. Staff have criteria for choosing equipment and books

12. Transition in and out of the setting is well established and effective

13. Planning is led by the interests and needs of the children who attend the setting

14. Children's views are sought both informally and formally especially regarding individual targets

15. Each parent/carer feels valued by practitioners; their views and opinions are regularly sought

16. The setting has a vision and ethos which includes meeting the needs of those children with additional needs

17. The setting is well organised with good policies and procedures in place

18. All children are equally welcome to attend

19. Staff have developed sound methods of communicating with parents

20. Procedures are in place to support staff to identify children who may have an additional need

Starter quiz
How inclusive is your pre-school?

1. Is your Pre-school used by a **wide cross-section** of the local community?
   - (a) Yes
   - (b) A few
   - (c) Not really

2. Do you have links with local schools and other Pre-schools in your neighbourhood?
   - (a) Yes
   - (b) Some
   - (c) Not really

3. Do you link with health visitors and other health care professionals such as speech and language therapists?
   - (a) Yes
   - (b) Sometimes
   - (c) Never

4. Do your staff receive training on special needs or inclusion issues?
   - (a) Yes
   - (b) Sometimes
   - (c) No

5. Do you have a SENCO who has allocated time to carry out their duties?
   - (a) Yes
   - (b) Have a SENCO but they have no allocated time
   - (c) No

6. Are all staff confident in identifying children who may have additional needs?
   - (a) Yes
   - (b) Some of them
   - (c) No

7. Is your planning differentiated to include children who may have additional needs?
   - (a) Yes
   - (b) Sometimes
   - (c) No

8. Do you talk to the children about what they do and involve them in planning activities?
   (a) Yes
   (b) Sometimes
   (c) No

9. Do you meet regularly with parents to discuss progress and exchange information?
   (a) Yes
   (b) Not often
   (c) No

10. Are staff and parents aware of your Special Educational Needs/Inclusion Policy?
    (a) Yes, both are
    (b) Staff aware, parents not
    (c) Neither are aware

11. Do your displays represent society and your local community in all its diversity?
    (a) Yes
    (b) Usually
    (c) No

12. Do you have a clear criterion for choosing new books, toys and resources?
    (a) Yes
    (b) A rough guideline
    (c) No

Scoring

For each answer (a) score 3 points; answer (b) score 2 points; answer (c) 1 point.

Score between 28 and 36

★Gold star awarded – you are well on your way be becoming a fully inclusive setting. This book will help you go the extra mile.

Score between 20 and 27

★Silver star awarded – you are half way there! Well done. This book will help you to clarify your ideas and plan for the future.

Score between 12 and 19

★Bronze star awarded – you still have quite a long way to go. HOWEVER, you have made a good start by consulting this book. We are sure you will find the following ideas and suggestions helpful. Go for it!

Hands-on activities

1   Use the insights you have gained in Chapter 1 to discuss and/or write an inclusive Admissions Policy for a Pre-school.

During an Ofsted inspection you are asked about your arrangements for caring for children with special needs.

2   Devise an answer using the list of '20 ways to recognise an inclusive setting'.

As a group see if you can offer several positive answers to this question.

Look at the 'Starter quiz – how inclusive is your setting?' Check your results.

3   Write a five-point action plan which will enable you to achieve a better score next time.

Discuss within your staff group how you can implement these changes.

Imagine that you were interviewing prospective staff for your Pre-school setting.

What would you tell them about your staff team's attitudes to inclusion?

4   What question would you ask them in relation to how they would support this positive ethos?

Use the 'Everyone benefits from inclusion' section to help you do this.

 Further reading

Allez, A., Arnott, G., Henderson, A. and Toff, M. (1996) *Equal Chances*. London: Pre-school Learning Alliance.

Department for Education and Skills (DfES) (2001) *National Day Care Standards*. London: DfES.

Department for Education and Skills (DfES) (2003) *Day Care: Guidance to the National Standards – Revisions to Certain Criteria*. London: DfES.

Department for Education and Skills (DfES) (2004) *Every Child Matters: Change for Children*. London: DfES.

Nutbrown, C. and Clough, P. (2006) *Inclusion in the Early Years*. London: Paul Chapman Publishing.

CHAPTER TWO

The legislation: what it means for you

The aim of this chapter is to explain and address issues raised for pre-schools by the Disability Discrimination Act 1995 and Code of Practice for Special Educational Needs (DfEE, 2001). From September 2002 the Disability Discrimination Act 1995 (DDA) applies to all providers of early years services.

This information will be invaluable to practitioners and owners of Pre-school settings. Students, tutors and advisers will find it a useful backdrop from which to consider inclusion policies and practice.

The chapter sets out:

▶ A definition of disability

▶ The law and you – your legal obligations

▶ What the DDA looks like in practice

▶ Expectations resulting from the Code of Practice

▶ Sample Inclusion Policy

▶ The role of the SENCO

It also offers suggestions for additional activities designed to build on the topics covered in the chapter, and a list of recommended further reading.

How the DDA defines disability

A large group of children currently attending our Pre-school settings are covered by the duties of the DDA.

By definition a disabled child *also* has Special/Additional Educational Needs (SEN) if they need special provision to be made, in order for them to access the education and care that is available locally.

The definition of disability in the Disability Discrimination Act 1995 is:

> *a physical or mental impairment which has a substantial and long-term adverse effect on [a person's] ability to carry out normal day-to-day activities.*

However, *not all* disabled children have SEN. For instance, a child with hearing aids which bring their hearing up to within a normal range would be classified as having a disability but *not* a special educational need, as this is unlikely to affect their education.

Equally, some children with SEN will also be defined as having a disability under the Disability Discrimination Act 1995. For example, a child with significant behaviour difficulties which are caused by an underlying impairment could be defined as being disabled.

Your legal obligations

The DDA sets out two core duties:

> 1. Not to treat a disabled child '***less favourably***'
>
> 2. To make '***reasonable adjustments***' for disabled children
>
> From October 2004 *reasonable adjustments* includes removing physical barriers.
>
> The core duties are '***anticipatory***' and provision and plans for disabled children should therefore be in place before they might actually be needed.

These duties apply to all early years providers; however, there are differences in the way the duties apply to schools and to other providers.

Part 3 of the DDA covers:

▶ Day nurseries

▶ Family centres

▶ Pre-schools

▶ Playgroups

▶ Individual childminders

▶ Other forms of private and voluntary provision which are not schools

Part 4 of the DDA covers:

▶ All schools – private and independent, state maintained and mainstream or special provision

Failure to comply with these two core duties – treating a child 'less favourably' and not making 'reasonable adjustments' for disabled children – may amount to unlawful discrimination. This could lead to a claim being made to the County Court (Part 3 settings) or to the SEN and Disability Tribunal (Part 4 settings).

What the DDA looks like in practice

Treating a disabled child 'less favourably'

 Case study

Jacob is a child who has an autistic spectrum condition which sometimes affects his behaviour. The Pre-school has arranged an outing to the zoo. The children are excited and looking forward to going. At a staff meeting some practitioners express concern that it may be too dangerous to take Jacob as he has a tendency to run off. The manager of the setting explains to Jacob's parents that they won't be taking Jacob on the trip.

▶ In this case Jacob is being treated 'less favourably' as he is being left behind because of his difficult behaviour; however, his actions are a result of his condition.

▶ Practitioners do have genuine concerns that need to be addressed but they also have a responsibility to make efforts to include Jacob. There are very few instances where it is not possible to include a child if practitioners have an open mind and there is sufficient planning. In this case practitioners could have

   – prepared Jacob thoroughly for the trip

   – arranged for an extra member of staff to accompany the group

   – asked Jacob's parents if they want to join the trip – his parents are not obliged to do this, however.

Making 'reasonable adjustments' for disabled children. From October 2004 'reasonable adjustments' includes removing physical barriers.

 Case study

Mary is three years old and has a condition that makes getting around difficult. She can walk but finds it very difficult to use stairs. Her difficulty becomes obvious when she and her parents have a pre-admissions visit to the Baby Bear room which is upstairs in the setting. Following the visit practitioners meet and agree that Baby Bears  should be moved into a downstairs room so that Mary would not have to negotiate the stairs and would have easy access to the garden.

▶ Practitioners have been inclusive and have made 'reasonable adjustments'. They have not been able to make changes to their building but have found a practical solution to the challenges they faced.

Planning for 'anticipatory duties'

 Case study

A Pre-school setting decided to review all of its policies especially the admissions policy to ensure that it was not discriminating against children who may have a special need. Adjustments were made and a reference to children being toilet trained before starting nursery was removed.

▶ The practitioners in this setting showed that they were clearly planning for anticipatory duties. They were thinking ahead and ensuring that they did not discriminate against any children.

For help in auditing your setting and planning ahead see the 'Taking stock' sheets at the end of Chapters 3 and 4 and on the CD-ROM that accompanies this book.

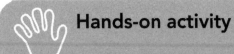

Hands-on activity

Harry is 16 months old and has a visual impairment. He started at the Pre-school when he was 9 months old and now he is quickly becoming an active toddler. Harry has recently begun to crawl around the room and staff expect that he will soon be walking. A specialist teacher for the visually impaired visits Harry at home.

What 'reasonable adjustments' would you expect to make within your pre-school to support Harry's inclusion?

Who could support you to make these adjustments?

An invaluable booklet for practitioners in helping to explain your legal duties is

Early Years and the Disability Discrimination Act 1995: What Service Providers Need to Know, published in 2003 by the Council for Disabled Children, Sure Start and the National Children's Bureau (NCB). Copies are available from NCB book sales (Tel: 020 7843 6029 or email: booksales@ncb.org.uk; ask for EYSENDA/03).

Expectations resulting from the Special Educational Needs Code of Practice 2001

The Code of Practice (DfEE, 2001) outlines certain expectations in regard to all stages of a child's education. These begin in the early years, and Pre-school practitioners and settings are expected to 'have regard' to them.

These expectations include a series of principles that Pre-school settings are expected to adhere to, as well as references to policies and procedures.

The principles of the Code of Practice

▶ Every child with special educational needs should have their needs met

▶ As far as possible these needs will be met within a mainstream setting with access to a broad, balanced and relevant curriculum

▶ The views of parents should be sought and taken into account

▶ Wherever possible, the views of the child should be taken into account

Pre-school settings are expected to apply the above basic principles to their everyday *policies, practices and procedures*.

Pre-school settings are *specifically* required to:

▶ Have a Special Educational Needs or Inclusion Policy

▶ Appoint a named SENCO to be responsible for the day-to-day operation of the Special Educational Needs or Inclusion Policy

The following pages address these two requirements and give an example of:

▶ an Inclusion Policy which can be customised to suit your Pre-school setting

▶ an outline of the role of the SENCO in the Pre-school, as stated in the Code of Practice. This could form the basis of a job description for your SENCO.

Sample Inclusion Policy

Here at

.... we
want all of our children to have the best possible learning opportunities and
experiences. We welcome and actively promote inclusive practices and diversity within
our setting. Our aim is to make our setting accessible to all families who wish to use it.
We have due regard to the Special Educational Needs Code of Practice 2001 and
comply with the requirements of the Disability Discrimination Act 1995.

Within our Pre-school we endeavour to provide an inclusive environment and curriculum
that enables all children to fully participate in the activities and experiences on offer. We work
in partnership with parents and other agencies, where appropriate, to support individual
children's learning. We aim to provide effective support to meet every child's needs.

Our Manager and Special Educational Needs Co-ordinator (SENCO) are
responsible for the implementation and annual review of our Inclusion Policy. They
ensure that all staff, students and parents are aware of the policy and we welcome
discussion about individual children or any other matters arising from the policy.

Our present SENCO is ....
and he/she is responsible for the day-to-day organisation of any matters regarding
children with special/additional needs. It is, however, the responsibility of all staff to plan
for, work with and support all children whatever their needs.

Early identification

▶ Through our record keeping and comprehensive system of regular observations we
are able to recognise any additional needs a child may have. We always in the first
instance discuss any concerns with parents and together plan an appropriate course
of action and support. This will be regularly monitored by our SENCO.

▶ Children who have an identified additional need on joining the setting will be welcomed
and celebrated in the same way as all of our children. An individual settling-in plan will
be devised by staff and parents. Suitable levels of support will be offered and input and
advice from other agencies and professionals will be sought. The SENCO will take
responsibility for co-ordinating this – working closely alongside parents.

Intervention

▶ In line with national and local procedures, we monitor progress carefully using the
graduated response outlined in the Code of Practice. This includes a systematic cycle
of assessment, planning, action and review.

▶ We liaise closely with parents and seek advice on the sorts of things their children like
to do, as well as listen to their priorities in regard to their child's progress. We aim to
achieve progress by using the child's strengths and interests as our starting point.

▶ We record clear targets for children and develop strategies to ensure progress and
learning. This may take the form of an Individual Education Plan (IEP). We encourage
parental and child participation in devising these targets and action plans.

- We liaise closely with local education authority (LEA) advisory staff and make effective use of any LEA funding and resources, such as staff training; this helps us meet the identified needs of the children in our Pre-school.

Our inclusive practices include:

- Ensuring that all children participate in the daily routines of the setting while maintaining a flexible approach.
- Encouraging all children to take part in activities/experiences at their own level and pace. This includes both indoor and outdoor play and any trips undertaken.
- Offering open-ended learning activities and experiences using differentiation as the basis of all planning.
- Using a range of strategies to engage children in play and learning. We provide activities to suit children's most effective learning style.
- Ensuring that all children's contributions and efforts are treated positively by staff and that achievements are celebrated.
- Arranging respectful privacy for children's personal care.

This policy links to our other Pre-school policies, specifically:

- Admissions
- Health and Safety
- Equal Opportunities
- Working with Parents and Carers

Signature of Manager: ...*Ann Hodson*...

Signature of SENCO: ...*Mary Mitchell*...

Date of policy: ...19.6.06...

The Role of the Special Educational Needs Co-Ordinator (SENCO)

The Code of Practice clearly lays out the role of the Special Educational Needs Co-ordinator or SENCO. (In some cases the title has been changed to Inclusion Co-ordinator or INCO.)

The SENCO role is one which carries a great deal of responsibility and careful thought needs to be given to who, in the Pre-school, is best placed to fulfil that role.

The Code of Practice also suggests that consideration is given to the amount of time which could be reasonably allocated to enable a SENCO to carry out their duties effectively.

The SENCO is responsible for:

▶ The *day-to-day organisation* and running of provision for children with special or additional needs.

▶ *Record keeping* – making sure that relevant background information about individual children is collected, recorded and updated.

▶ *Advising* – supporting other practitioners in the setting.

▶ *Planning* – helping to plan the support for individuals in discussion with colleagues.

▶ *Documenting* – ensuring that appropriate Individual Education Plans (IEPs) are in place and being carried out.

▶ *Monitoring* – through observation and reviewing any actions or plans.

▶ *Liaising* – creating links and dialogue between parents and other professionals in respect of children with special educational needs.

The Code of Practice does make it clear, however, that *all* staff are responsible for working with and supporting children with special or additional needs. Key workers who usually have responsibility for working with a child on a daily basis should continue to do so. This will naturally include observing, planning and delivering individualised programmes and keeping parents informed and consulted.

Some documentation which may help the SENCO meet these responsibilities is included in Chapter 5 and Appendix A and can be found on the CD-ROM accompanying this book.

 Hands-on activities

Write a job description for a SENCO in a Pre-school setting.

Use the description of the role of the SENCO given above and Chapter 4 of the Code of Practice for Special Educational Needs (DfEE, 2001) to help you.

1

2

What do the following mean?

▶ DDA

▶ SEN

▶ SENCO

Use this list to begin your own glossary of terms used in relation to legislation and the Code of Practice.

What are the two core duties of the DDA?

3

Being a pre-school SENCO brings many responsibilities and rewards. Write a list of 5 characteristics needed to be a good SENCO.

1. Being well organised

2.

3.

4.

5.

4

Using this chapter, remind yourself which settings are covered by:

▶ Part 3 of the DDA

▶ Part 4 of the DDA

What section does your setting come under?

 Further reading

Department for Education and Employment (DfEE) (2001) *Special Educational Needs Code of Practice*. London: DfEE.

Mortimer, H. (2001) *Special Needs in Early Years Provision*. London: Continuum.

Practical Pre-school (2002) *Special Educational Needs in Practice*. Leamington Spa: Step Forward Publishing.

Pre-school Learning Alliance (2002) *The Role of the Special Educational Needs Co-ordinator in Pre-school Settings*. London: Pre-school Learning Alliance.

CHAPTER THREE

The setting: creating an inclusive environment

The aim of this chapter is to help you take stock of your pre-school and give practical advice and examples of how to improve accessibility and plan for the future. Through doing this you will be well on your way to fulfilling your obligations in respect of current disability legislation.

Owners and managers will find this chapter helpful when assessing new premises or improving their current provision. Practitioners are provided with practical, easy-to-make adjustments to enable them to include all children. Students and tutors can use this chapter as a means to measure the accessibility of the physical environments they visit. Advisory teachers will find it a useful tool to use when supporting Pre-schools to improve and plan for greater inclusion.

The step-by-step guide in the chapter sets out:

▶ What you can do – practical suggestions for things you can do to improve accessibility

▶ Ideas to try – changes you can make to different areas of your Pre-school

▶ How to take stock and plan for the future – use the 'Taking stock' and 'Accessibility plan' sheets provided to help you reflect on your provision.

The chapter also offers suggestions for additional activities designed to build on the topics covered, and a list of recommended further reading.

Creating an inclusive environment

It is recognised that no two Pre-school settings are the same; they range from school nurseries, children's centres and independent schools to community groups. Some are housed in purpose-built premises and offer full day care to babies, toddlers and young children. Others may be local groups operating from rented premises such as church halls or community centres, offering part-time provision.

Every setting has a unique combination of circumstances including physical environment, management structure, budget and resources. Wherever the setting it is possible to meet the challenge of creating an inclusive and accessible environment for children, staff, parents/carers and visitors.

The following steps will help you begin to create an inclusive environment:

Step 1

What you can do

Read the practical suggestions for making your Pre-school more accessible.

Step 2

Ideas to try

Look at some basic changes you can make to each area of your Pre-school.

Step 3

Audit your provision

Reflect on your provision and use either the blank diagram sheet (page 40) or the 'Taking stock' and 'Accessibility plan' sheets (page 41 and 42) to help you plan to improve each area.

Getting to know you

The key words to remember when admitting children into your Pre-school setting are *preparation* and *flexibility*.

Practitioners are all too aware of the need for adequate preparation for all children starting Pre-school. This should be reflected in all aspects of practice, from the time that an application is made, to the child's first day at the setting.

Many parents and carers of children with additional needs are especially anxious about making the right choice of Pre-school provision and leaving their child for the first time. It is therefore important to promote your ethos as an open and inclusive environment.

What you can do

▶ **Have a well-designed admissions form**
Effective planning can only be done thoroughly when information from parents and carers is full and accurate. A good admissions form can gather all the information that is needed and help plan the settling-in process, as well as any action that needs to be taken before a child starts.

▶ **Have a standard 'settling-in' procedure**
This should be known to all parents. It should have built-in flexibility to allow for individual needs. Some children, for example, may need reduced hours or parental support for a period of time. Parents too find it reassuring to know that, as far as possible, their child and circumstances will be accommodated as a matter of course.

▶ **Ensure that training and/or any specialist equipment is in place before a child with additional needs starts at the Pre-school**
In order for a placement to be positive and successful, ideally any additional provision should be put in place before a child starts at the Pre-school. Where a child's needs are significant, additional information will need to be obtained from health or education professionals already involved with the child. Professionals will often offer guidance or training to whole-staff teams on specific individual needs.

Getting to know you

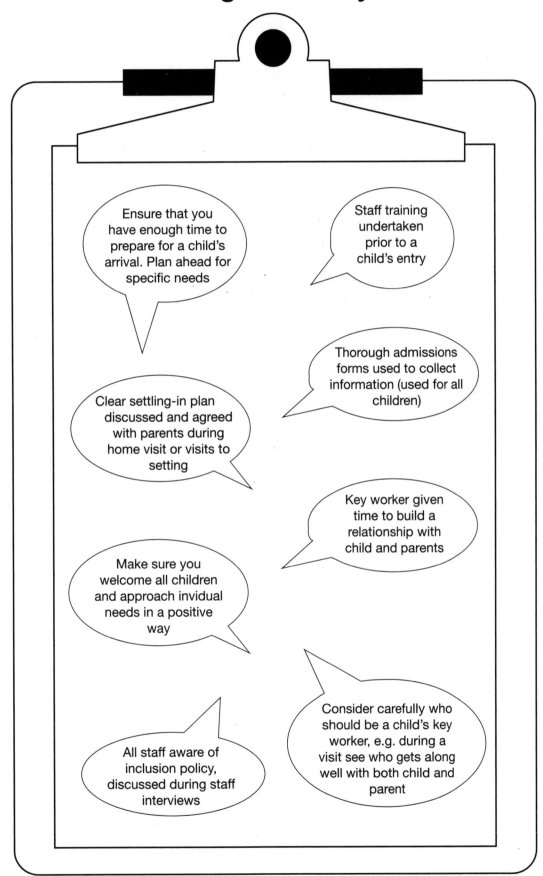

Ensure that you have enough time to prepare for a child's arrival. Plan ahead for specific needs

Staff training undertaken prior to a child's entry

Thorough admissions forms used to collect information (used for all children)

Clear settling-in plan discussed and agreed with parents during home visit or visits to setting

Key worker given time to build a relationship with child and parents

Make sure you welcome all children and approach invidual needs in a positive way

All staff aware of inclusion policy, discussed during staff interviews

Consider carefully who should be a child's key worker, e.g. during a visit see who gets along well with both child and parent

Hello and goodbye

Feeling welcome is important to all of us. When you make an effort to let children and their carers know that they are welcome you are building a foundation of trust and mutual respect.

The physical environment, especially the entrance of a Pre-school, sends an important message to everyone who enters the building. Staff in most Pre-schools are well aware of this and every effort is usually made to make families feel as welcome as possible.

What you can do

▶ Make the effort to personally welcome all children into the Pre-school.

▶ Ensure you have displays and notice boards for information about the day's activities, pictures of staff, daily menu, etc.

▶ If you share premises, use a movable board, or a small room divider or a notice board that fits onto wall hooks, removing them at the end of sessions.

▶ Have bright and uncluttered entrance ways and identify a storage place for children's buggies.

▶ Try to provide ramps for all nursery users, useful for buggies as well as wheelchairs. Discuss the purchase of a temporary ramp or even something more permanent with other centre users or landlords.

▶ Signposts are particularly helpful and both entrance and exit signs should be clearly written and well lit. Makaton signs could be used to supplement the written word. Parents are a useful resource when it comes to having dual language signs.

▶ Exits and especially fire exits should always be clear with no furniture or equipment nearby.

▶ All staff and children should be aware of fire procedures and fire drill practice should take place regularly at various times of the nursery day. Remember to consider the safety of wheelchairs users, children, staff or parents with any additional need during fire drills. Even if you have no children with additional needs in your setting, one day you might.

Remember: **first impressions do count**.

Hello and goodbye

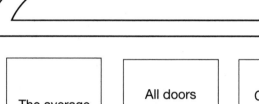

The average wheelchair needs an 800 mm opening for ease of access	All doors should have door closers for safety. Adjust to the minimum resistance for ease of opening	Check with your local authority advisers about the availability of a temporary ramp
Entrances and exits should be free from obstructions	Doorways should be adequately lit and signposted.	Mark glass doors with stickers to ensure visibility
Check doors for ease of opening. Consider height, grip and security	Handles and hand rails are more visible in a contrasting colour	The gradient of any ramp must comply with building regulations

Under your feet

Flooring is one of the most basic areas of your setting to consider. At the very least it should be clean, safe and preferably non-slip when wet.

Floors are best kept simple and plain, providing contrasting colours to the walls and doors.

What you can do

▶ Differences in levels can be highlighted using a change of colour or surface material such as carpet or cushion flooring.

▶ Steps or stair edges should always be highlighted. This is particularly useful to those with visual impairments but also benefits those children who are still a little unsteady on their feet or just beginning to negotiate steps. You can have professionally installed rubber trims or simply use coloured tape, as long as it is secured properly and checked regularly for wear.

▶ Delineating areas using different flooring is also both useful and practical. Carpet or matting can create a quiet area for sharing books and serves the dual purpose of absorbing sound, so reducing noise levels which some children (and staff!) find distressing.

▶ Individual mats can be useful tools in directing children to particular 'spots' on the carpet at story time for example. This can often improve behaviour and concentration. Carpet samples are a very cheap and sometimes are a free resource!

▶ For more messy activities there are now commercially available non-slip mats which can be placed under sand or water trays and these may be a good investment if you are a setting in a multi-purpose building.

Under your feet

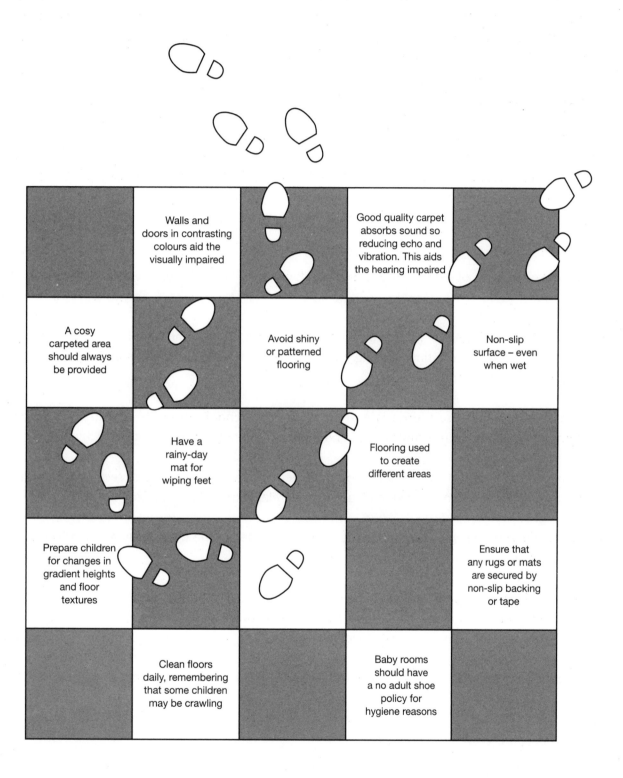

	Walls and doors in contrasting colours aid the visually impaired		Good quality carpet absorbs sound so reducing echo and vibration. This aids the hearing impaired	
A cosy carpeted area should always be provided		Avoid shiny or patterned flooring		Non-slip surface – even when wet
	Have a rainy-day mat for wiping feet		Flooring used to create different areas	
Prepare children for changes in gradient heights and floor textures				Ensure that any rugs or mats are secured by non-slip backing or tape
	Clean floors daily, remembering that some children may be crawling		Baby rooms should have a no adult shoe policy for hygiene reasons	

Light and bright

A bright and airy room filled with natural light is the ideal for all Pre-school settings. Unfortunately the reality is sometimes very different for some settings who often find themselves in dual-purpose rooms with little natural light. Even in such circumstances improvements can be made.

What you can do

▶ Consider carefully the layout of a room and plan to make the most of any natural light.

▶ Use blinds or curtains to adjust light. If this is not possible, tape up temporary pieces of net curtain or use sheets of tissue paper to diffuse the light.

Ideas to try

▶ To make the most of available light keep windows clean and any lighting free from dust and dirt.

▶ Have a long-term view of your Pre-school's decoration programme. Think about decorating one area of a room at a time. Use light and warm shades such as creams and light blues to help create a calm atmosphere.

▶ Use colour shades to differentiate areas of the Pre-school. Similarly consider choosing complementary or contrasting colours and textures for flooring and furniture.

▶ Light dimmers can be very useful especially when children are sleeping or resting during the daytime. They can also be used to create a more relaxed mood during story sessions.

▶ Stairs and toilets need to be particularly well lit as these are the most likely accident spots in any nursery.

▶ Advice about the needs and requirements of individual children, particularly those with visual impairments, can be obtained from local authority advisory staff and health care professionals. Advice is often very specific and specialist.

Remember: never be afraid to ask for help and advice from LEA advisory staff or parents.

Light and bright

Be aware of areas which may lie in shadow. Ensure suitable lighting especially if children are reading or mark making	Light may need to be adjusted throughout the day by using curtains, blinds or nets. Avoid glare in your setting	Remember: painting window glass or covering with children's work can negatively affect lighting in a room
A room's natural light should be used to its full potential	Bulbs and others lighting need to be cleaned regularly to keep them free from dust	When transferring between light and dim conditions, some children will need time to adapt to the new light
Wall colourings are best kept neutral and calm		When talking to a whole group it is important to position yourself, with the light falling on your face, so that all of the children can see you clearly

In, on and under

A tidy and uncluttered environment is generally beneficial to all children. Careful thought needs to go into planning the layout of a room and before purchasing what is often expensive, new furniture.

All the ideas below are suitable for the whole nursery but where specialist equipment or furniture is needed for a particular child, it is wise to consult with any professionals involved before making any purchases.

Physiotherapy or occupational therapy departments and local authority staff often have items that they can loan to parents, carers and settings.

What you can do

▶ Ensure that main routes and pathways around the setting and between activities are clear of obstructions and wide enough for a wheelchair to pass easily.

▶ Have storage units that enable children of various heights, including those who may be reaching from a wheelchair or buggy, to gain access to toys and equipment.

▶ Kidney-shaped and transparent sand and water trays are preferable to the standard rectangular shape as they allow children to see what is inside as well as providing enough space for a chair or wheelchair to be pushed underneath.

▶ Use a variety of words, colours, signs and pictures to label drawers and cupboards. This allows children more independence in choosing activities and also helps at tidy-up time!

▶ When buying or replacing furniture consider buying a variety of different heights. Most manufactures offer matching chairs and tables of varying heights and at least one should accommodate a wheelchair.

▶ Look out for chairs offering extra support for children for whom sitting is difficult. These often take the form of animal shapes and are very appealing.

▶ Different colour furniture and storage can be useful to delineate areas of the Pre-school.

▶ Remember to ensure that all edges are rounded for safety.

In, on and under

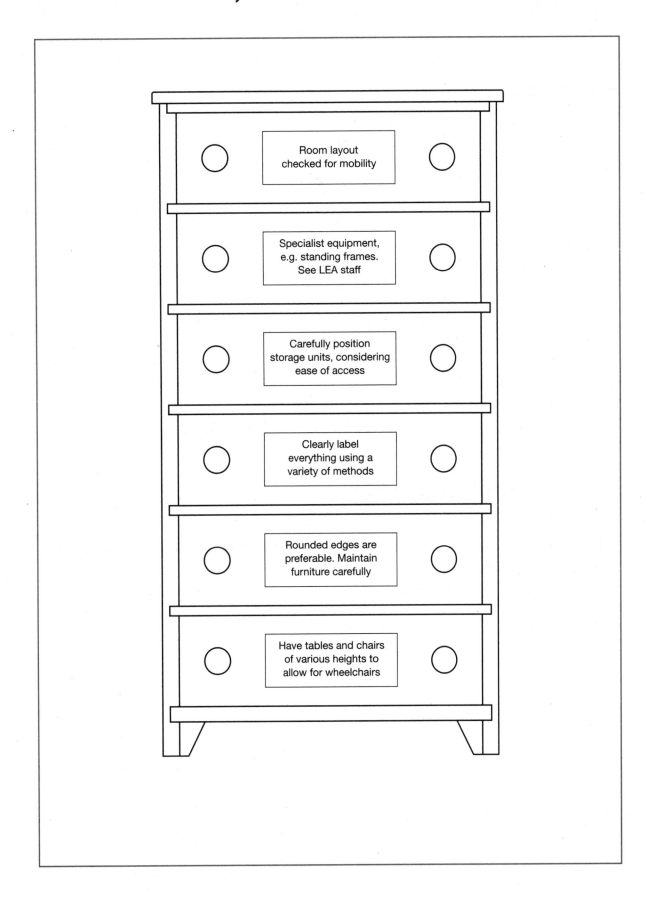

Room layout checked for mobility

Specialist equipment, e.g. standing frames. See LEA staff

Carefully position storage units, considering ease of access

Clearly label everything using a variety of methods

Rounded edges are preferable. Maintain furniture carefully

Have tables and chairs of various heights to allow for wheelchairs

Playing out

Changes to outdoor areas can range from very simple adjustments to larger projects, such as creating a sensory garden, providing large-scale play equipment adapted for wheelchairs or specialist play surfaces.

Whatever your situation, improvements can be made given some thoughtful planning.

What you can do

▶ Divide up larger spaces to create different areas of activity such as a climbing area, other large equipment area, quiet spaces, and shady places.

▶ Use carefully placed seating or rows of planting boxes to divide up these spaces.

▶ Turn some pathways into tracks for bikes, cars or other push-me-pull-you type equipment.

▶ Make the most of naturally occurring features, such as the often neglected brick wall. It can, for example, be turned into a visual and tactile experience for very little cost, using everyday and recycled items available from DIY/furniture stores.

▶ Clear, wide and uncluttered pathways help those with poor motor skills, those in wheelchairs and those who are visually impaired.

▶ Regular maintenance, especially in terms of litter and gardening tasks, should be a matter of daily routine.

▶ Handrails can be relatively inexpensive yet make a huge difference for some children.

 Hands-on activity

As a team or in small groups go to your outside area without children. Look at the area through the eyes of a child with walking difficulties.

What do you see?

How can you improve the area to suit this child?

Activities outdoors should always be carefully planned and viewed as an extension of the indoors.

Playing out

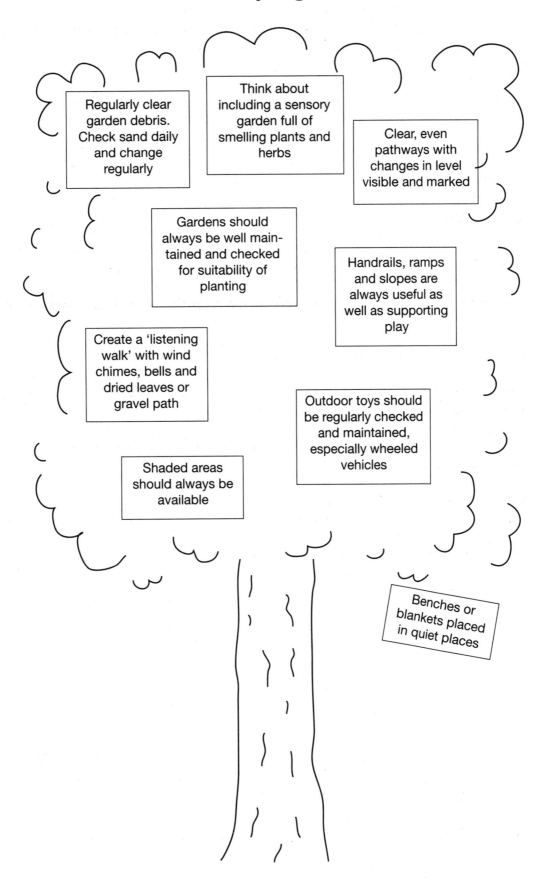

Regularly clear garden debris. Check sand daily and change regularly

Think about including a sensory garden full of smelling plants and herbs

Clear, even pathways with changes in level visible and marked

Gardens should always be well maintained and checked for suitability of planting

Handrails, ramps and slopes are always useful as well as supporting play

Create a 'listening walk' with wind chimes, bells and dried leaves or gravel path

Outdoor toys should be regularly checked and maintained, especially wheeled vehicles

Shaded areas should always be available

Benches or blankets placed in quiet places

Clean and fresh

The key to successful personal care for all children is that staff arrange for respectful privacy and ensure that children are treated with dignity and sensitivity. With many younger children now attending Pre-school settings most practitioners are familiar with nappy changing and toileting procedures.

Staff should be expected to take 'reasonable steps' to support children who have extra toileting needs.

It is against the sentiments of the DDA for any setting to refuse entry to a child who is not completely toilet trained.

What you can do

▶ Practitioners need to be provided with clear guidelines for toileting procedures. This is especially important in the case of children with additional needs.

▶ Make sure you ask parents to share information regarding their child's toileting habits and routines used at home.

▶ Staff should have access to disposable gloves and aprons.

▶ There should be facilities for the disposal of nappies and all nappy changing areas should be wiped clean after use.

▶ Toilet and washroom areas should be clean, bright, and fully equipped with hot water, liquid soap and either hand dryers or paper towels.

▶ Adaptations such as toilet steps and toilet seat insets should be provided either by the setting or with advice by specialist professionals.

▶ Where space is limited consider using a wall-mounted pull-down type changing unit.

All settings should include in their accessibility plan the installation of a disabled toilet if they don't already have one.

Clean and fresh

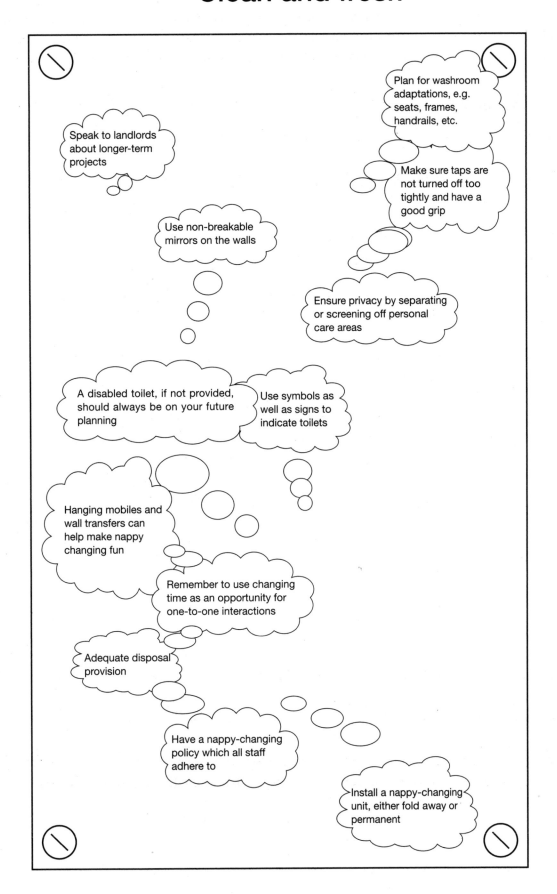

Plan for washroom adaptations, e.g. seats, frames, handrails, etc.

Speak to landlords about longer-term projects

Make sure taps are not turned off too tightly and have a good grip

Use non-breakable mirrors on the walls

Ensure privacy by separating or screening off personal care areas

A disabled toilet, if not provided, should always be on your future planning

Use symbols as well as signs to indicate toilets

Hanging mobiles and wall transfers can help make nappy changing fun

Remember to use changing time as an opportunity for one-to-one interactions

Adequate disposal provision

Have a nappy-changing policy which all staff adhere to

Install a nappy-changing unit, either fold away or permanent

Safe and healthy

Children are best kept at home when poorly and staff should not be put under pressure to admit a child who is clearly unwell. This is especially the case in day care settings. Clear procedures and guidelines should be in place and shared with parents to ensure this does not happen.

What you can do

▶ Named first aiders should always be available throughout the Pre-school session.

▶ Train staff in the use of any procedures or administration of medication prior to the child/ren arriving at the Pre-school.

▶ Two members of staff should be present when medication is given. A note should always be made of the date, time and amount administered.

▶ Situate medicine cupboards well out of the reach of children. Practitioners should note if medicine needs refrigerating.

▶ Ensure that medical conditions or allergies are known about prior to admission in order for snack procedures etc. to be reviewed.

▶ Health Care Plans should be in place for children with identified medical needs. Advice can be obtained from health care professionals and they should be involved in the writing of any plan.

Note: *Medicine forms and Health Care Plans can be found in the DfES/Department of Health document listed in the 'Further reading' section at the end of the chapter.*

The sharing of information regarding a child's health is an important first step in keeping children safe.

 Hands-on activity

As a team or in small groups use the local library facilities or the internet to:

▶ Identify plants that might be common to the garden but are poisonous

▶ Find out what medical conditions could be affected by animals that a pre-school setting may keep, or those who may use the outdoor garden when the nursery is not in use

Ideas to try

Safe and healthy

Accident books should be kept up to date and available to all staff. Be prepared to share these with parents

Check your First Aid box does not contain out-of-date materials. Individual children's medicines should be clearly labelled, and refrigerated if necessary

Ensure regular staff training for First Aid and any individual child specific health needs

Make sure all staff are aware of any child with an allergy

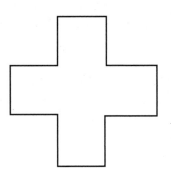

Write procedures for snack time and use of food, taking account of any allergies children have

Any child with a medical need should have a Health Care Plan in place ideally before the child attends the setting

Staff should be aware of and respect issues of confidentiality. There should be close liason with parents

And finally ...

It is probably obvious by now that every aspect of a Pre-school setting is affected by issues of inclusion and our last section highlights just a few of those remaining areas.

What else you can do

Staff

▶ Existing and newly appointed staff should be aware of the setting's inclusion policy and how this is put into practice.

▶ There should be an appointed person, usually a Special Needs/Inclusion Co-ordinator who is responsible for the everyday running and organisation of this policy.

▶ The employment of staff who themselves may have additional needs should be considered and all recruitment and advertising should comply with DDA legislation.

▶ Ongoing training of staff with regard to special needs issues is also important and courses offered by local authorities as well as private organisations should be fully utilised.

▶ Issues of confidentiality is another area which should be discussed in whole-staff teams. A procedure should be established for what happens to and who is told sensitive information.

▶ Parents have the right to ask setting managers to keep information confidential and this right has to be respected. It is important, then, to have established good relationships with parents to be able to work together.

▶ Practitioners should take account of every child's right to be included. Some policies, including those for trips and outings, need particular thought; however, with careful choices, risk assessment and planning there is no reason why there should be any difficulties.

Parents

▶ Remember that some parents may have individual needs that are not always immediately apparent. Difficulties with literacy in particular can cause embarrassment and help may also be needed for those with English as an additional language.

▶ Communications and documents of all kinds should be available in alternative formats. Taped information is always useful not only for those with additional needs but also for busy parents who would prefer to listen to information as they drive to work or do the ironing!

Ideas to try

And finally ...

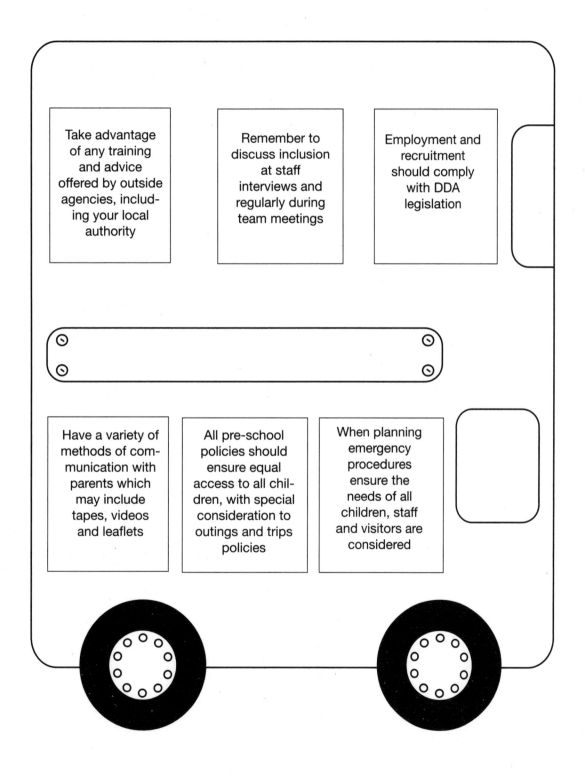

Take advantage of any training and advice offered by outside agencies, including your local authority

Remember to discuss inclusion at staff interviews and regularly during team meetings

Employment and recruitment should comply with DDA legislation

Have a variety of methods of communication with parents which may include tapes, videos and leaflets

All pre-school policies should ensure equal access to all children, with special consideration to outings and trips policies

When planning emergency procedures ensure the needs of all children, staff and visitors are considered

Step 2

Use this sheet to look at basic changes you can make to an area of your Pre-school

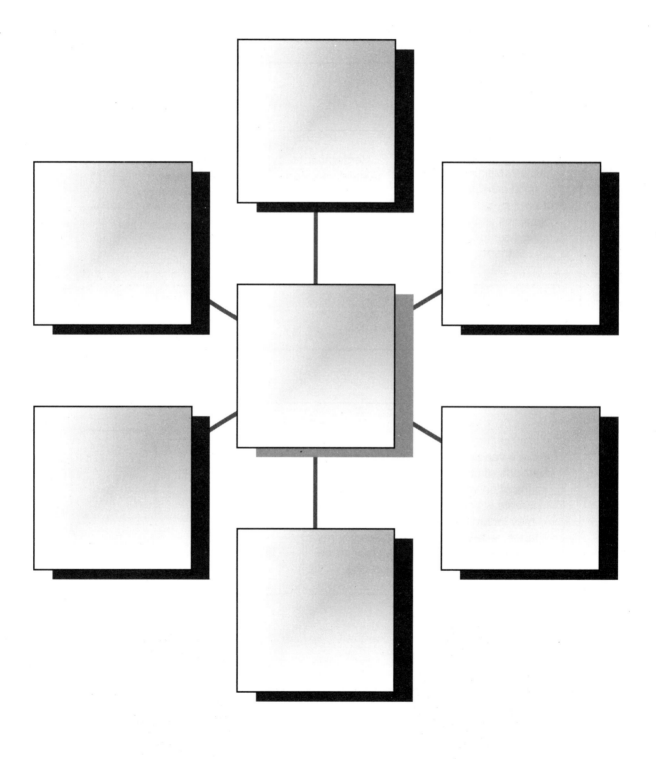

A Practical Guide to Pre-school Inclusion. Paul Chapman Publishing © Chris Dukes and Maggie Smith

Step 3
Taking stock of accessibility in your setting

Area of the setting to be considered: _____ Date: _____

Things to change or improve

Time span	What and by whom	Cost	☺
In the next month			
In the next year			
In the next 2 years			

Step 3

Accessibility plan

Short/Medium/Long term

Date ....

ACTION/S NEEDED / TO BE COMPLETED BY	ESTIMATE OR COST £	EVALUATION/TO CONSIDER NEXT
SECTION/AREA		
SECTION/AREA		
SECTION/AREA		

A Practical Guide to Pre-school Inclusion. Paul Chapman Publishing © Chris Dukes and Maggie Smith

Hands-on activity

Consider the changes you may have to make to your environment to accommodate the following children.

To help you, look at each of the areas discussed in this chapter.

▶ Consider the physical environment, staff interventions and who you could ask for advice.

Brian

Brian is a three-year-old boy who uses a walking frame to aid mobility. He loves to access all areas of the pre-school and is particularly keen on playing outdoors.

Sarah

Sarah is a two-year-old child who attends your setting. She has a visual impairment. Her condition may get worse. Sarah loves books and story times.

Priya

Priya finds it very hard to sit still; she is constantly on the move and has little sense of any danger. Priya has a habit of getting out of the room and playground.

Simon

Simon has allergies to some foods and various outdoor plants. He has an inquisitive nature and loves to try out new things.

Annabel

Annabel is a child who has to take many different kinds of medicine to stay healthy. Her mother is anxious about leaving her as she needs medicine administered throughout the day.

▶ What kind of planning should be carried out before these children start at your setting?

 Further reading

Department of Education and Skills (DfES)/Department of Health (2005) *Managing Medicines in Schools and Early Years Settings*. London: DfES

CHAPTER FOUR

Play and learning: creating inclusive opportunities

The aim of this chapter is to illustrate how to create a successful play environment and how to become a supportive play partner. It shows Pre-school practitioners how to make areas of the nursery and equipment more accessible to all children.

This information will ensure that owners, managers and practitioners offer high quality learning opportunities to all children. Students, tutors and advisers will find the ideas a useful starting point when discussing how to set up a successful Pre-school setting environment. It will also be a useful basis for developing planning and evaluation skills.

The step-by-step guide in the chapter sets out:

▶ Why? – looking at each area of the Pre-school and why it is important for the development of children with additional needs

▶ What is your role? – practical ideas on what to do and how to be a supportive play partner

▶ Ideas to try – tips to improve activity areas and equipment

The chapter also offers suggestions for additional activities designed to build on the topics covered in the chapter, and a list of recommended further reading.

Play and children with Special/Additional Educational Needs

All children need to experience high quality play experiences. Some may find play activities more difficult than others to access. Communication problems, physical barriers and learning difficulties can all provide an extra challenge for young children and Pre-school practitioners alike.

Children should have the opportunity to participate in all types of activities and experiences through which they learn how to choose, share and co-operate. In doing so they become part of the Pre-school community as a whole and can make friendships that can last for years. Children with additional needs *will* want to access the same types of activities as their peers. It should be made possible for them to do this.

Through training and experience Pre-school practitioners know that children learn best through play. Helping children to develop a range of play and learning skills requires self-confident staff who are prepared to 'go the extra mile'. The aim for practitioners is to support children without taking over the child's agenda. *Play always belongs to children*, but practitioners can help children to develop their play.

The following steps will help you provide inclusive play experiences:

Step 1

Why?

Read and remind yourself why inclusive play opportunities are important.

Step 2

What is your role?

Reflect on what kind of play partner you are and consider the ideas suggested to help you develop your practice.

Step 3

Ideas to try

Look at the diagrams to audit the activity areas and equipment in your setting. Use either the blank diagram sheet (page 40) or the 'Taking stock' and 'Inclusion plan' sheets (pages 66 and 67) to help you plan and improve these areas.

Books and the book corner

Why?

Through looking at books together children learn about themselves, the world around them and each other. Sharing books is the ideal opportunity for children with additional need to work co-operatively with their peers.

Staff should select books carefully, making sure they open children's eyes to the world as well as showing them that they themselves are part of the wider community.

Young children need to find out that reading is fun. It is a pleasurable activity that can be shared with others or carried out by themselves. This means that Pre-schools need to invest in a wide range of materials both fiction and non-fiction. The very nature of books ensures differentiation so it is good practice to expose children to as wide a range as possible. Consider the message your books give to children and parents with additional needs. Ensure your choice of books helps people to feel included and fully represents the diverse community.

What is your role?

▶ Provide a quiet, cosy, carpeted area with a comfortable chair or cushions. Make sure the books are on display and accessible to all children.

▶ Provide a wide range of books such as picture books, tactile books, non-fiction books, pop-up books, lift-the-flap books, poetry and nursery rhymes, big books and listening books or story tapes as well as visual props and a story sacks.

▶ Teach book-handling skills, bearing in mind that some children will find this a difficult skill to learn. Board books or fabric books can be a good starting point.

▶ Encourage participation by reading repetitive and favourite books that encourage children to join in and read along.

▶ Talk about pictures in books with children; encourage children to predict or tell their own story.

▶ Purchase books that show a good overview of society and deal with issues of disability sensitively and in a factually correct way.

▶ Use the public library to ensure a variety of new or different books.

▶ Create opportunities for children to share books – one holding the book and the other helping to turn the pages.

▶ Create a listening corner, which allows children to listen and learn together and provides access to books in a different format.

▶ Use small world equipment for illustration when telling stories to benefit children who need visual cues.

Ideas to try

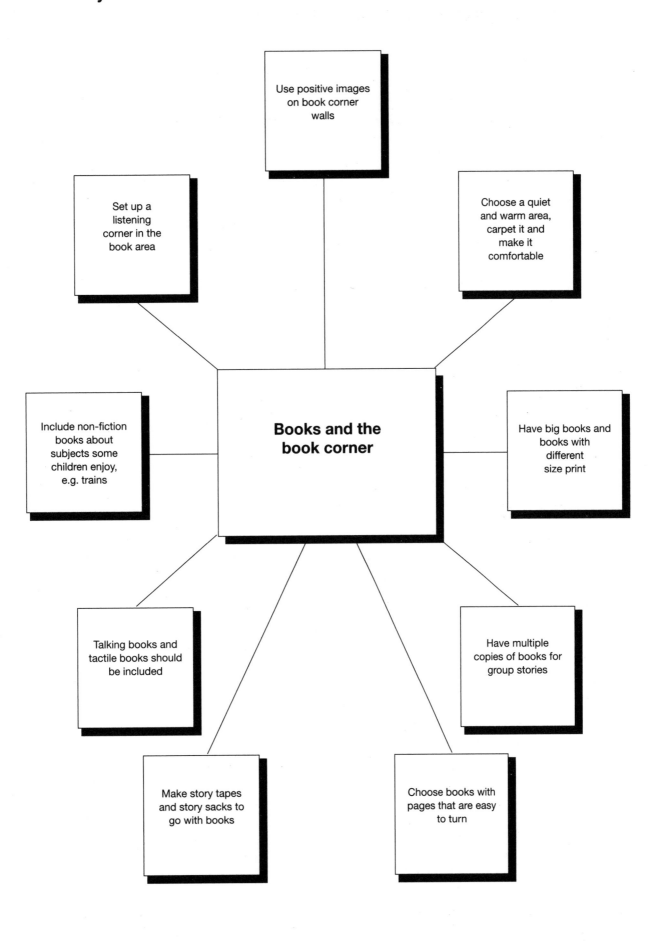

Use positive images on book corner walls

Set up a listening corner in the book area

Choose a quiet and warm area, carpet it and make it comfortable

Include non-fiction books about subjects some children enjoy, e.g. trains

Books and the book corner

Have big books and books with different size print

Talking books and tactile books should be included

Have multiple copies of books for group stories

Make story tapes and story sacks to go with books

Choose books with pages that are easy to turn

Mark making and creative activities

Why?

The importance of mark making and creativity has been recognised over recent years. Children are encouraged to express themselves and are no longer expected to produce pieces of work using templates created by practitioners.

Children with additional needs often have strong ideas and great imaginations, but they can be easily frustrated if they are unable to communicate verbally. Some children need to be able to explore other means of expressing themselves. Mark making and creative areas provide an ideal opportunity to do this.

Through activities such as painting, working with clay and junk modelling children are developing many skills. They are beginning to make choices, develop language skills, develop hand–eye co-ordination, co-operate and share as well as beginning to appreciate colour and texture and form.

What is your role?

▶ Create a workshop area with imaginative resources accessible for all children to reach, take and use, keep tidy and well stocked.

▶ Encourage children to return to a piece of work later, accepting that some children find concentrating difficult.

▶ Have an unfinished work tray and regularly check through it.

▶ Put up a soft, low notice board with large-headed pins, as well as a shelf nearby, for children to display their work. Thick cork wall tiles are good to use.

▶ Offer the children who need it support to handle materials by being an 'extra pair of hands'.

▶ Be directed by the child and try not to offer too many suggestions.

▶ Encourage creativity but with the emphasis on doing rather than the end product.

▶ Create a relaxed atmosphere where children can enjoy each other's company and be creative.

Ideas to try

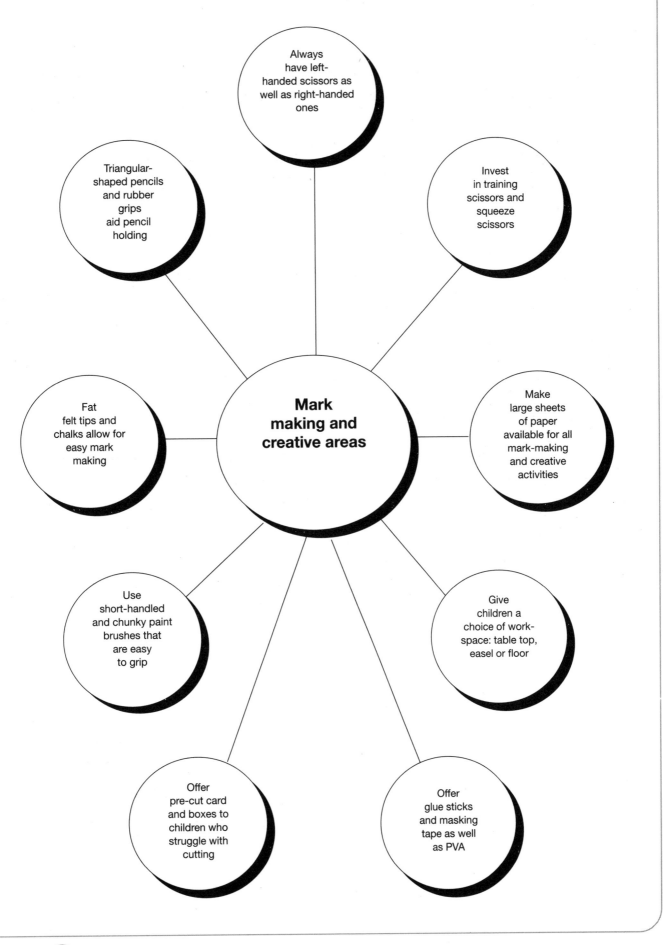

Always have left-handed scissors as well as right-handed ones

Triangular-shaped pencils and rubber grips aid pencil holding

Invest in training scissors and squeeze scissors

Fat felt tips and chalks allow for easy mark making

Mark making and creative areas

Make large sheets of paper available for all mark-making and creative activities

Use short-handled and chunky paint brushes that are easy to grip

Give children a choice of work-space: table top, easel or floor

Offer pre-cut card and boxes to children who struggle with cutting

Offer glue sticks and masking tape as well as PVA

Construction and building activities

Why?

Some children respond naturally to the challenge offered by using construction and building materials. Others need to be encouraged and supported by practitioners to gain the best out of this type of play.

Through the use of construction and building activities children develop many skills such as selecting and using a variety of materials, developing concentration, mathematical concepts, and the ability to assemble and organise materials.

In short children are in charge of the outcomes of their own efforts and ideas. When working with children with additional needs, the challenge is to help them achieve the outcomes they have pictured in their own imagination. This requires practitioners who are inventive, skilful and adept at supporting children.

What is your role?

▶ Create a quiet, well-resourced workshop area with plenty of space.

▶ Show children suitable images that will inspire creativity.

▶ Offer children an appropriate working space – this could be cushions on the floor for support, or materials on a tray in front of children. Be on hand to help replenish equipment.

▶ Work alongside children, providing encouragement and physical support in their chosen work area, e.g. floor or table top. Take your lead from them – say, 'What should I do'?

▶ Be on hand to facilitate and guide the sharing of equipment and the protection of unfinished models.

▶ Allow children to return to their work by making safe their efforts on a shelf.

▶ Celebrate achievements – show models at circle times; use a digital camera to share with parents their child at work.

▶ Build upon a child's strengths and preferences; use this knowledge when providing materials.

Ideas to try

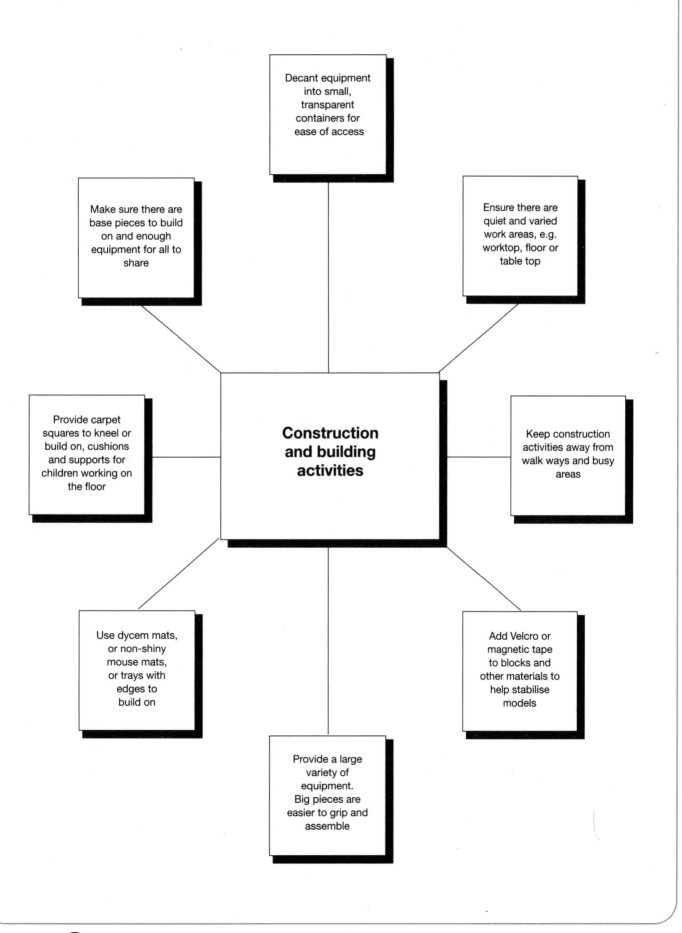

Decant equipment into small, transparent containers for ease of access

Make sure there are base pieces to build on and enough equipment for all to share

Ensure there are quiet and varied work areas, e.g. worktop, floor or table top

Provide carpet squares to kneel or build on, cushions and supports for children working on the floor

Construction and building activities

Keep construction activities away from walk ways and busy areas

Use dycem mats, or non-shiny mouse mats, or trays with edges to build on

Add Velcro or magnetic tape to blocks and other materials to help stabilise models

Provide a large variety of equipment. Big pieces are easier to grip and assemble

Imagination, music and carpet time

Why?

Within all Pre-school settings children spend time playing imaginatively, making music and participating in carpet time activities. Children's feelings of belonging and being part of the nursery community are developed during these times.

Although invaluable some children find these sessions difficult. Children with additional needs may find participation at carpet time hard as they struggle to sit still, listen or communicate their ideas. Similarly, the imaginative experience offered by free play can be a challenge to children who have underdeveloped play and social skills.

What is your role?

▶ Support stories and the learning of new songs and rhymes with visual props.

▶ Make sure all children, especially those who may need support, can access an adult.

▶ Ensure all children can see the book/prop during story and singing sessions.

▶ Do not expect all children to sit for the same amount of time during sessions; be flexible and offer alternative activities or smaller groups.

▶ Some children may need their own place to sit during story times; consider using carpet squares so that all children have enough or their own space.

▶ During news or circle time activities make sure all children are given the opportunity to participate in their own way; always allow children time to respond (remember: waiting and silence is OK).

▶ Monitor and support children during imaginative play; this can be done discreetly by limiting numbers and helping children to access play equipment.

▶ Make sure that imaginative play equipment and resources reflect the wider society.

▶ Recognise that some equipment may need careful introduction and modelling of how to use it, e.g. musical instruments.

▶ Be aware that some children may be sensitive to noise or over-stimulated by lots of activity. A quieter alternative could be offered.

▶ Appreciate that some children will need adult support or direction to participate fully.

Ideas to try

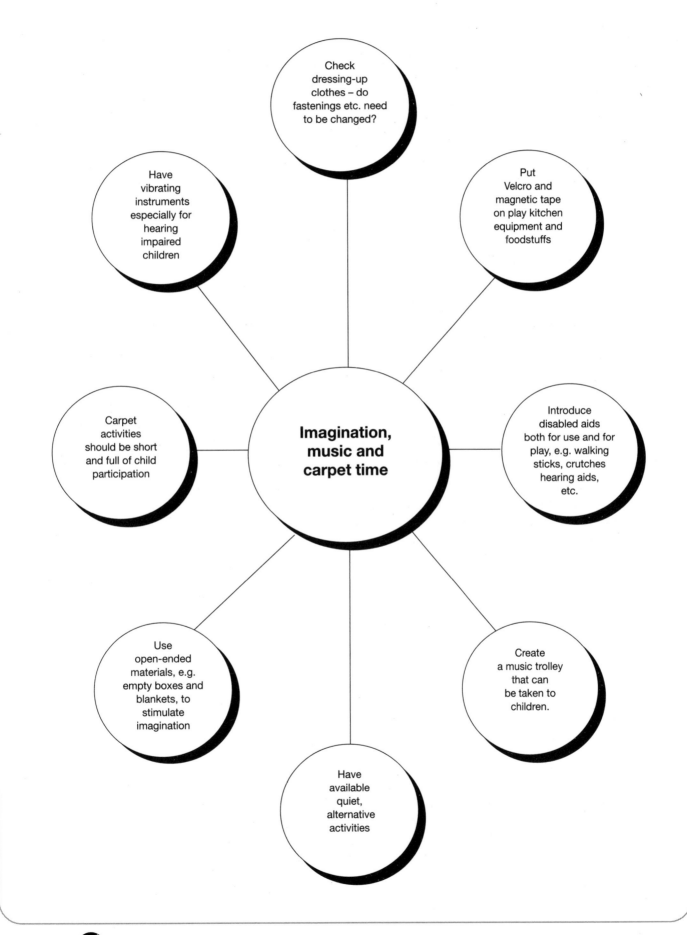

Check dressing-up clothes – do fastenings etc. need to be changed?

Have vibrating instruments especially for hearing impaired children

Put Velcro and magnetic tape on play kitchen equipment and foodstuffs

Carpet activities should be short and full of child participation

Imagination, music and carpet time

Introduce disabled aids both for use and for play, e.g. walking sticks, crutches hearing aids, etc.

Use open-ended materials, e.g. empty boxes and blankets, to stimulate imagination

Create a music trolley that can be taken to children.

Have available quiet, alternative activities

Information and Communications Technology

Why?

The use of computers, digital cameras and video is as common in Pre-school settings as it is in many homes. It is something familiar to even the youngest children. All forms of Information and Communications Technology (ICT) can benefit children whatever their individual needs. For some children it may be the only way to access learning.

Computers are a great way to capture a child's interest. Many games and activities are highly motivating and multi-sensory in content. Children find it a non-threatening way to learn new skills. The computer can provide opportunities to practise or repeat skills and to build concentration in an enjoyable and fun way.

Most software is accessible at different levels – differentiation is in-built and all children can experience success. Children have an element of independence when using the computer which undoubtedly boosts confidence and self-esteem. Many programs also have reward systems such as on-screen animation, music or certificates which can be printed out.

What is your role?

▶ Allow children to access the computer independently during free choice time.

▶ Create opportunities for children to work together in pairs or in small groups, each working to their own strengths and learning from each other.

▶ Provide interactive software that develops skills such as problem solving, making choices and language acquisition.

▶ Ensure that the correct seating and keyboard positions are adopted. If a child has physiotherapy or occupational therapist involvement, seek their advice about computer adaptations.

▶ Check software content is representative of a diverse society. Consider drawing up your own checklist of criteria for use when purchasing software (see choosing toys and resources checklist on page 65).

▶ There is a note of caution when using programs which generate sound, as some children with hearing impairments can find it painful unless they have suitable aids.

▶ For children who may use augmentative forms of communication such as Makaton or computer-generated support, there are programs which create the necessary signs and symbols. These have proved useful to all children who need additional visual cues.

Ideas to try

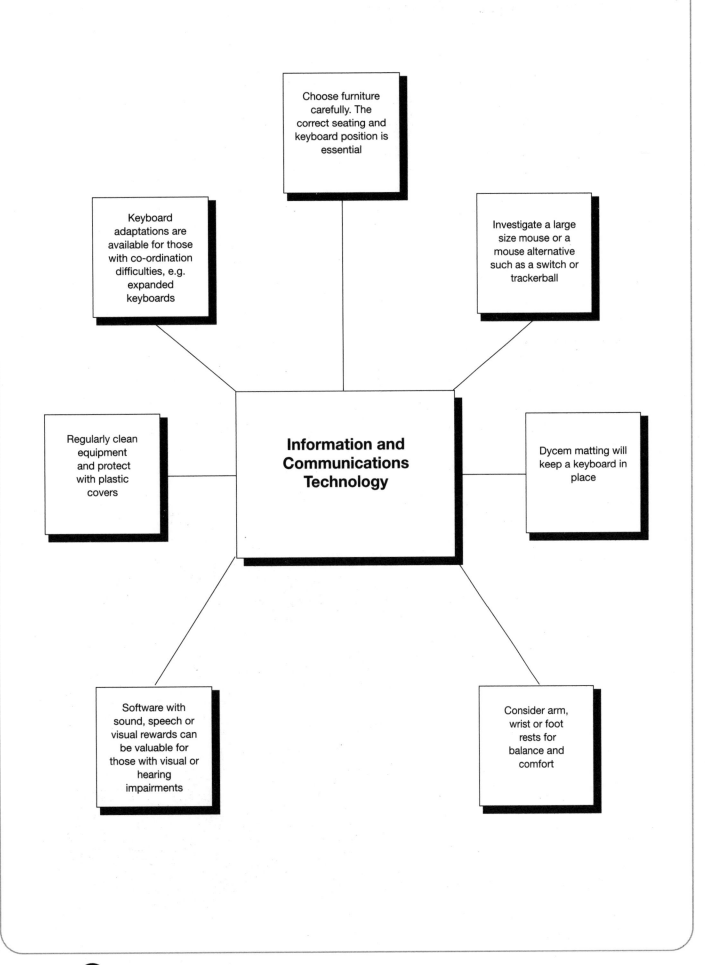

Choose furniture carefully. The correct seating and keyboard position is essential

Investigate a large size mouse or a mouse alternative such as a switch or trackerball

Keyboard adaptations are available for those with co-ordination difficulties, e.g. expanded keyboards

Information and Communications Technology

Regularly clean equipment and protect with plastic covers

Dycem matting will keep a keyboard in place

Software with sound, speech or visual rewards can be valuable for those with visual or hearing impairments

Consider arm, wrist or foot rests for balance and comfort

Table top and small world play

Why?

When working on table top activities children develop attention to detail, they practise small movements and build up their concentration skills and cognitive development.

Through practising activities such as threading, jigsaw puzzles and peg boards fine motor skills are refined, crossing the midline is practised and a pincer grip and two-handed co-ordination is developed.

Socially, children learn to co-operate with peers, take turns and share. Children develop staying power and emotional needs can be satisfied through the successful completion of activities.

Through the provision of small world toys and activities such as cars, trains, play people and animals, children are offered countless opportunities to develop imaginatively. They act out scenarios and develop their own sense of the world.

What is your role?

▶ Break activities down into small steps for those children who need extra support.

▶ Consider teaching some new activities like threading in different ways, analyse tasks and activities and devise several ways to teach new skills, e.g. for some children it is good to start threading with the child taking the beads off the thread, or the jigsaw pieces out of a completed jigsaw puzzle. Remember: not all children learn in the same way.

▶ Make sure children have the satisfaction of completing the last part of the activity, e.g. the final piece of a jigsaw, putting in the last peg, etc. (even if they have had a lot of support for the whole activity). This will help motivate children for future learning.

▶ Offer different levels of threading and peg boards from large and easy to do to those requiring greater fine motor skills.

▶ Grade your puzzles using a label on the back of the equipment.

▶ Think about adapting some equipment so children can handle it easier such as using kitchen roll holders and curtain rings to stack, or stiff straws to thread onto.

Ideas to try

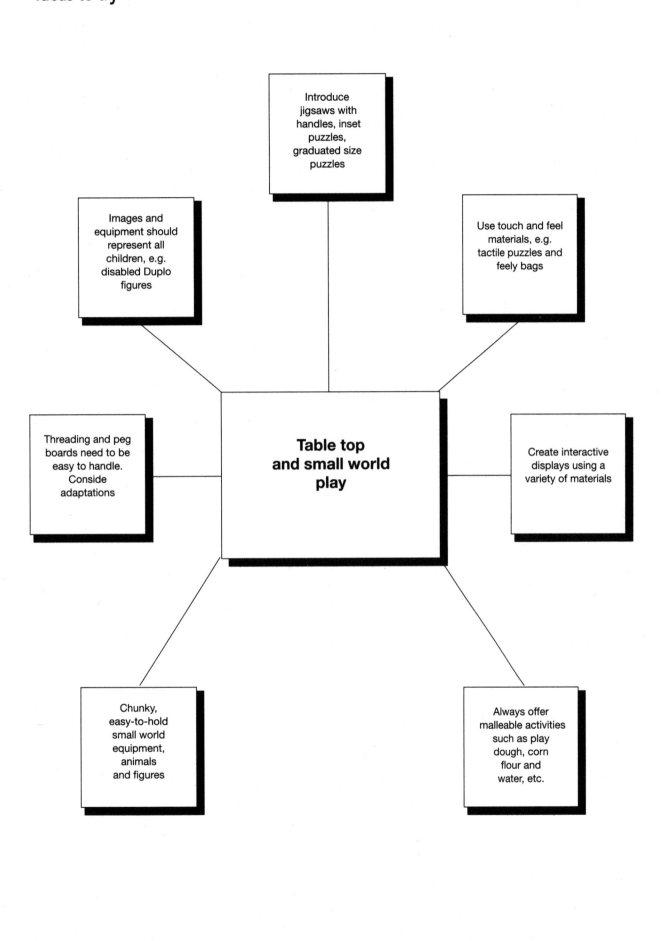

Introduce jigsaws with handles, inset puzzles, graduated size puzzles

Images and equipment should represent all children, e.g. disabled Duplo figures

Use touch and feel materials, e.g. tactile puzzles and feely bags

Threading and peg boards need to be easy to handle. Conside adaptations

Table top and small world play

Create interactive displays using a variety of materials

Chunky, easy-to-hold small world equipment, animals and figures

Always offer malleable activities such as play dough, corn flour and water, etc.

▶ Attach Velcro or magnetic tape to some equipment to help make it more manageable or to keep it in place.

▶ Offer an extra pair of hands to help hold or secure equipment while children work.

▶ Combine small world activities with sand and water or construction materials. This offers more depth and challenge.

▶ Place books and selections of natural materials such as wood or shells with small world activities to stimulate children's imagination and help develop play.

Malleable and messy play

Why?

These types of activities should *always* be made available. They provide children with the opportunity to explore and learn using their senses, develop language skills and become familiar with mathematical concepts such as volume and mass. These activities also provide a time when children have the chance to socialise and have fun!

Many children with additional needs have less opportunity to get messy in a natural way such as running in puddles, helping with cooking at home, etc. so it is important that Pre-schools allow them the chance to experiment. Practitioners need to be well organised and prepared to offer high levels of support in order for some children to access these types of activities.

What is your role?

▶ Make experiences appeal to different senses. Play dough with flavouring, colouring or perfume such as lavender oil gives the activity an extra dimension.

▶ Encourage children to discuss and predict what will happen when you add water or ice for example. Repeat the same activity with different materials.

▶ Introduce tools, cups, jugs and other equipment once children have had a chance to explore with their hands or feet first!

▶ Incorporate activities which use both hands at the same time to help develop two-handed co-ordination.

▶ Be well organised with bowls of soapy water and towels ready. Remember that some children will need help to clean themselves up.

▶ Some children dislike messy play and they should never be forced to do an activity. Always offer an alternative, let them watch and give them the opportunity to join in when they are ready.

Note: *It is important to remember that some children have allergies or sensitivity to certain materials and this should be thoroughly checked beforehand. Always ask about allergies on your admissions form. Children with severe allergies will need a Health Care Plan to ensure that there is an agreed procedure for dealing with any adverse reactions.*

Ideas to try

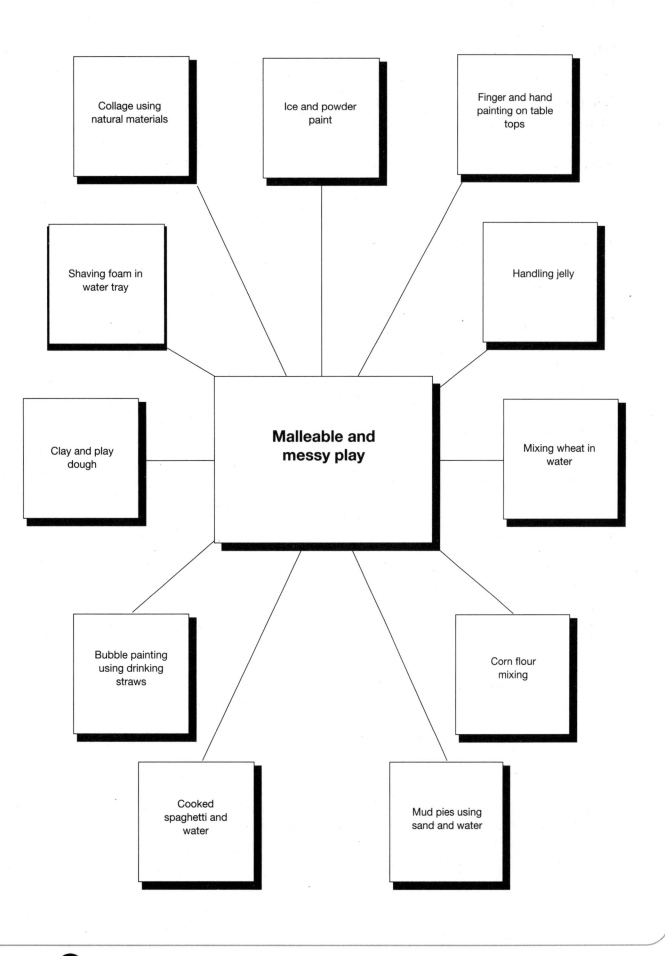

Collage using natural materials

Ice and powder paint

Finger and hand painting on table tops

Shaving foam in water tray

Handling jelly

Clay and play dough

Malleable and messy play

Mixing wheat in water

Bubble painting using drinking straws

Corn flour mixing

Cooked spaghetti and water

Mud pies using sand and water

Outdoor play

Why?

Outdoor play is essential for all children. Being out in the fresh air or in the sunshine with children is one of the greatest pleasures of working in the early years. If children are wrapped up warm on cold days and covered in sun cream on hot days, there is no excuse *not* to be outside. Indeed, given the choice some children would spend the entire time outdoors. It is important, then, that the outside is looked upon as an extension of the inside and careful consideration given to planning for inclusive outdoor play.

Although it is necessary to create an accessible environment and to provide a variety of appropriate equipment, the key element to inclusive play lies in the role of the practitioner. A sensitive and creative practitioner can make a world of difference between a child being included or not.

Children can, and should, be involved in planning outdoor activities. They always have ideas about how the outdoor area should be set up and are often more imaginative than the adults! It is also an excellent way of encouraging problem solving, promoting social interaction and developing language skills.

What is your role?

▶ Be prepared to make 'on the spot' changes. This could mean adjusting seating, moving or repositioning equipment.

▶ Where possible, anticipate and pre-empt those activities that some children may find challenging.

▶ Suggest or prompt games or tasks to make sure that every child has a role and to encourage children to work co-operatively.

▶ Follow the children's lead – ask what they would like to do and do what you can to make it happen.

▶ Guide those children who find the outdoor space worrying or intimidating by helping them to choose equipment or by suggesting ways to use it.

▶ With your support, encourage children to try something new. In this way they will be able to test themselves and their abilities in a safe and secure environment.

▶ Get involved! For some children an adult playing alongside is the only way they can access activities in a meaningful way. This might mean pushing a car that a child can steer but not pedal, hand-over-hand guidance to dig the garden, or sliding down the slide side by side.

Ideas to try

Obstacle courses with alternative routes can be accessed by all

Swings attached to climbing frames allow the less mobile to join in

Large junk materials, tyres, blocks and blankets encourage social play

Swings with adjustable height and back rest or safety straps are useful

Large play equipment

Trampolines and seesaws can satisfy those who need to repeatedly rock or jump

Double bikes, scooters and rockers allow children to share and help each other

Ball pools inflatables, foam mattresses and paddling pools provide sensory experiences

Double-width slides allow helpers to slide alongside

Wide ramps, platforms and slopes allow every-one to experience height

Ideas to try

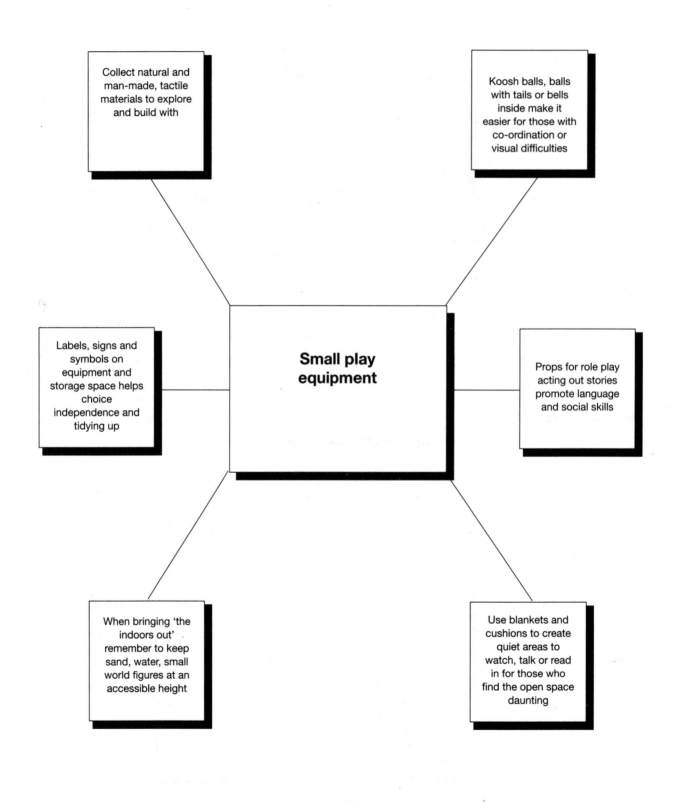

Collect natural and man-made, tactile materials to explore and build with

Koosh balls, balls with tails or bells inside make it easier for those with co-ordination or visual difficulties

Labels, signs and symbols on equipment and storage space helps choice independence and tidying up

Small play equipment

Props for role play acting out stories promote language and social skills

When bringing 'the indoors out' remember to keep sand, water, small world figures at an accessible height

Use blankets and cushions to create quiet areas to watch, talk or read in for those who find the open space daunting

Hands-on activities

Adam needs to develop his fine manipulative skills and his ability to use both hands together (two handedness). As a team or in small groups think of some ideas for suitable activities that he can do both at home and at Pre-school.

One activity could be:

▶ Two-handed handling and manipulation of play dough

Try to come up with some other ideas that would help Adam.

Look in some catalogues and choose a toy or piece of equipment that you may consider buying for your setting. Use the 'Choosing toys and resources checklist' on page 65 to see how suitable and flexible a resource it will be.

As a team or in small groups draw up a list of games and activities that can be used at carpet time to help children work together or begin to learn to take turns.

One game could be:

▶ Sing the 'Row the boat' song and perform the action with children working in pairs

Use more examples from your list.

How might you support children with additional needs to participate and enjoy?

Hands-on activities

All children need the opportunity to make decisions and choices for themselves. How would you support a child with speech and language difficulties to make choices?

1 One way could be:

▶ Drinks time – hold up two different drinks and encourage the child to choose by pointing at the one he/she wants

Use more examples you have thought of.

Books and the book corner

Using the ideas outlined in 'What is your role?' (page 46) design and plan for the ideal book
2 corner.

Include a list of essential equipment and a sketch of how it would look.

Highlight how this area would benefit a child with a hearing impairment.

Malleable and messy play

Plan suitable activities for a child with multiple allergies (including wheat).

3 Write a short plan of how you would introduce and carry out one of the activities, paying particular attention to the organisation needed.

Use the ideas outlined in 'What is your role?' (page 58) to help you.

Outdoor Play

Aysha is a child who loves to be outdoors with her friends. She has trouble walking but can
4 crawl around quite fast. As her key worker how can you:

▶ Ensure Aysha experiences outdoor play?

▶ Ensure Aysha's safety while outdoors?

 Further reading

Casey, T. (2005) *Inclusive Play*. London: Paul Chapman Publishing.

Collins, M. (2001) *Circle Time for the Very Young*. London: Lucky Duck Publishing.

Drifte, C. (2002) *Early Learning Goals for Children with Special Needs: Learning through Play*. London: David Fulton Publishers.

Step 3

Choosing toys and resources checklist

Toy or resource	Yes	No	Other	
Does it offer the potential for co-operative play?				
Does it offer opportunities for social interaction?				
Does it appeal to the senses, e.g. does it have sound/movement etc.?				
Can it be used for more than one purpose?				
Is it attractive and appealing to all children?				
Will it offer challenges or leave a child frustrated?				
Is it easy to clean and store?				
Can parts be easily replaced?				
Is it suitable for use in different places, e.g. indoors and outdoors/floor or table top?				
Can it be used with items you already have to extend play opportunities?				
Does it allow for a child to use it and develop imaginatively?				
Does a child have to make choices?				
Does it offer a chance of success with no right or wrong way to use it?				
Is it safe and strong?				
Is it easy to manoeuvre, lift, drag or carry?				
Could you borrow one from a toy library to try out first?				
Will the manufacturer offer a trial or sample?				
Have you checked out all the alternatives?				

Note: This list is not exhaustive and can be added to.

Step 3

Taking stock of inclusive play opportunities in your setting

Area of play to be considered: .... Date: ....

Things to change or improve

Time span	What and by whom	Cost	☺
In the next month			
In the next year			
In the next 2 years			

Inclusive play plan   Short/Medium/Long term   Date ....

ACTION/S NEEDED / TO BE COMPLETED BY	ESTIMATE OR COST (£)	EVALUATION/TO CONSIDER NEXT	
AREA/ACTIVITIES			
AREA/ACTIVITIES			
AREA/ACTIVITIES			

CHAPTER FIVE

Making it happen: working with individual children and parents

The aim of this chapter is to help you plan for children's individual needs. It looks firstly at the tools which are already available to help you with planning and differentiation such as *Curriculum Guidance for the Foundation Stage* and the *Birth to Three Matters* framework. It then takes a more detailed look at the arrangements that should be made for children with special or additional needs. It will guide you through the various stages that are part of the 'graduated response' described in the Code of Practice for Special Educational Needs.

This is essential information for all practitioners, especially Pre-school SENCOs and managers. Students, tutors and advisers will find this chapter a clear introduction to creating a practical framework for inclusion.

The chapter sets out a step-by-step approach to planning for, and working with, individuals. This includes:

▶ Observations

▶ Collecting information

▶ Working with parents

▶ Writing Individual Education Plans (IEPs)

▶ Managing IEPs

▶ Child participation

▶ Outside support advice and assistance

In addition it provides a case study to illustrate the use of the proformas presented in the chapter. It concludes by offering suggestions for additional activities designed to build on the topics covered, and a list of recommended further reading.

Back to basics

The Birth to Three Matters framework

Birth to Three Matters: A Framework to Support Children in their Earliest Years (DfES, 2002) has been written to support those practitioners working with children and babies from birth to 3 years.

For some children aged 3–5 years, who are perhaps at earlier stages of development than might be expected for their age, this framework offers sound advice on how to support them in their development. Practitioners should feel comfortable using this framework to support these older children.

The framework covers four aspects which are then subdivided into smaller components and includes a range of activities and guidance on effective practice.

Curriculum Guidance for the Foundation Stage

When working with Pre-school children who are developmentally age appropriate, *Curriculum Guidance for the Foundation Stage* (QCA, 2000) offers ideas and structure.

The 'Stepping Stones' provide guidance for practitioners on how to provide support for children at different stages and help practitioners plan for differentiated activities.

Most practitioners will by now be familiar with the six areas of learning outlined in the document.

The Early Years Foundation Stage

The Early Years Foundation Stage (EYFS) is a new single framework that will bring together both the *Birth to Three Matters* framework and *Curriculum Guidance for the Foundation Stage* as well as some elements of the Day Care Standards. It will cover children from birth to the August following their fifth birthday.

For further information about the EYFS, look at the Sure Start website at www.surestart.gov.uk/publications.

Differentiation

Differentiation is an essential factor in enabling children with additional needs to access the early years curriculum. Put simply, differentiation means teaching a child in ways and at a level which match their individual learning requirements.

Practitioners should aim to do this by approaching activities in a way that will:

1. Provide the same types of experience for all children whatever their learning needs.

2. Give opportunities for children of different abilities to work and play together.

Remember: inclusion is not a child working individually on tasks which are different from his/her peers. It is a child working alongside others each making progress in his/her own way.

Alongside the curriculum and guidance documents, the other most important way of learning about a child's individual needs is through *observation*. Regular observations are routinely carried out in most Pre-school settings. Watching children play, interact and participate in a variety of activities can provide a wealth of information about their strengths and needs.

A planning cycle such as the one illustrated below can help you to begin to plan for individual needs.

When differentiation is not enough

Some children, despite having a differentiated curriculum, continue to have difficulties in making progress.

▶ It is then necessary to make plans and provision which is **additional to** or **different from** that which is made for most other children.

▶ These children could be described as having **special** or **additional needs**.

▶ The practices and procedures which should be followed are laid down in the Code of Practice for Special Educational Needs (DfEE, 2001).

◗ Chapter 4 of the Code is specific to early years settings and is summarised in the following pages.

What do we mean by 'Special Needs'?

The legal definition of SEN (Education Act 1996) as set out in the Code of Practice (DfEE, 2001, p. 6) is:

Children have special educational needs if they have a *learning difficulty* which calls for *special educational provision* to be made for them.

Children have a *learning difficulty* if they:

a) have a significantly greater difficulty in learning than the majority of children of the same age ...; or

b) have a disability which prevents or hinders them from making use of the educational facilities [to be found locally] for children of the same age ...;

c) are under compulsory school age and fall within the definition at (a) or (b) above or would do so if special educational provision was not made for them.

Special educational provision means:

a) For children of two and over – educational provision which is additional to or different from what would generally be provided.

b) For children under two – educational provision of any kind.

The Code of Practice describes **special educational needs** as falling into four main areas:

◗ Communication and interaction

◗ Cognition and learning

◗ Behavioural, emotional and social development

◗ Sensory and physical

Some children, of course, will have difficulties in more than one of these areas.

What if a child's first language is not English?

It is important to note at this point that while children who have English as an additional language may need extra support to develop their language skills, this in itself is *not* regarded as a special need.

> Children must not be regarded as having a learning difficulty solely because the language or form of language of their home is different from the language in which they are taught. (DfEE, 2001, p. 6)

Sometimes a child has English as an additional language as well as a special need. This is often difficult to assess. The starting point, however, should always be to gather information about how well the child is developing in his/her home language/s. The importance of working alongside parents and finding ways to communicate with them cannot be stressed enough. Establishing links with community groups is often a helpful way for settings to be able to provide support for parents as well as children.

If there is any doubt about a child's language development, help should be sought from outside professionals such as speech and language therapists. They are often able to arrange for dual language assessments to be carried out.

What next?

The Code of Practice sets out very clearly the procedures to be followed once a child is identified as having special or additional needs. The importance of both parental involvement and child participation are key principles in this process.

The actions which follow are part of a *graduated response* as shown in the planning cycle on page 70.

A graduated response

STEP 1

In the first instance it is presumed that all children have the benefit of a *differentiated curriculum*.

It is recognised that for a small number of children, this is not enough to enable them to make 'adequate progress'. Practitioners, parents or both together may express concern about a child's progress. In this instance practitioners should move to Step 2.

STEP 2

Gather *information* about the nature of the child's difficulties.

a) Carry out *observations*

These observations focus on particular areas of concern and are different in style to those routinely used by many Pre-school settings. They are between 15 and 20 minutes long and unlike a narrative observation do not record everything that the child does. Instead, they have a particular focus depending on the nature of the concern.

For example, where there is concern about a child's language development, the practitioner would write down everything that the child says or does not say in any interaction or situation. In this way very specific information can be gathered about the nature of the child's difficulties.

Arguably the most important part of the observation takes place after it is completed. It is then that staff should consider what they have observed and note down anything which seems significant. This information can then be used to inform planning and action that needs to be taken.

(See 'Observation Sheet' and 'Observation Follow-up' on pages 74 and 75.)

b) Meet with *key workers/staff*

Staff will have direct, everyday knowledge of the child. Many settings have a key worker system which allocates the care of particular children to particular members of staff. This can make for easier systems for observation and planning.

All staff, however, will have dealt with the child, have a different relationship with them and possibly see them, from a different perspective. The key worker should discuss concerns with the SENCO, but it is then important to talk as a staff group about any child causing concern.

Observation Sheet

Child's name:	Date:

Focus of observation:

<u>Time</u>	

A Practical Guide to Pre-school Inclusion. Paul Chapman Publishing © Chris Dukes and Maggie Smith

Observation Follow-up

What was noticed

What this could tell us

What we should do next

Observed by: Discussed with:

STEP 3

Meet with *parent/carer* to discuss progress.

Working successfully with parents is often the key to working successfully with a child. Parents have a wealth of information about their child which can be invaluable when thinking about strategies to help them.

Meetings should take place in a quiet area away from other parents and at a pre-arranged time, so that proper time and thought is given to the meeting.

It is important to handle the discussion in a sensitive and sympathetic way, with opportunities to talk about the positives as well as the difficulties.

The emphasis should always be on the child's best interests and ways forward in supporting them.

Generalisations are very unhelpful in these situations. Remember to be specific about your concerns. It is useful to have some notes and your observations to take with you to illustrate your points (see 'Parental Meeting Record' on page 77).

When you have gathered all the information together and have met with parents you will be ready to move to Step 4 and start planning for the individual needs of the child

---

Golden rules for working with parents

▶ Confidentiality must *always* be respected by *all* staff – *unless* a child protection issue is raised (then follow your child protection procedures).

▶ Consider the information you may have regarding a family – use it on a need-to-know basis and *always* with parental permission.

▶ Try to start all conversations with parents with a positive statement about their child.

▶ Develop good listening skills and keep interruptions to a minimum.

▶ Find a quiet, private place to talk and always make sure the parent has enough time, otherwise; schedule a meeting.

▶ Be tactful and let parents know you value and appreciate their child as well as their own input to the setting.

▶ Work on developing empathy with parents (put yourself in their place) and always thank them for their time.

▶ Make a dated note of relevant conversations or telephone calls you or other staff have with parents for future reference.

▶ Be respectful of child-rearing practices that differ from your own.

▶ If no translator is available for those who need one, ask parents to bring an English-speaking relative or friend with them to any meetings.

▶ Always discuss future plans with parents regarding their child; never have a meeting to discuss their child without informing them before the event.

Parental Meeting Record

Record of meeting with parent(s)   **Date:**

Child's name: **D.O.B.**

Present at meeting:

Reason for the meeting:

Information/What was discussed:

What should happen next:

Signed: (setting)   **Signed:**   (parent)

STEP 4

An *Individual Education Plan (IEP)* is written by the setting (see 'Individual Education Plan', page 83).

This identifies the areas in which the child needs to develop. Two or three very specific targets are set and strategies and resources are identified to help the child meet the target.

Target setting is not as easy as it sounds! Practitioners should concentrate on specific tasks. The child's success should be measurable and resources and strategies made explicit. In this way progress is easy to assess.

Good targets are often referred to as being **SMART**:

S – **Specific**

M – **Measurable**

A – **Achievable**

R – **Realistic**

T – **Time bound**

For example, if you would like a child *to be able to share and play with other children*, the target may be:

▶ to play a turn-taking game

▶ with one other child and the key worker

▶ for 10 minutes each day

▶ using the shopping and bus stop games

▶ with one person taking the turn wearing a hat

The child is said to have an IEP at 'Early Years Action' and all intervention or support is carried out 'in house'.

As a result of the Individual Education Plan, 'additional' or 'different' support is given to the child. This is usually carried out by the key worker as part of the everyday planning and provision in the setting. Some settings prefer to keep a running log of progress towards these targets. This can make it easier when reviewing an IEP.

(See Appendix A. 'Weekly Record of Progress Towards Targets'.)

IEPs and working with parents

Working in partnership with parents is essential. Parents should be invited to a meeting to discuss the Individual Education Plan. It is important that they are encouraged to be involved and contribute to the plan. Many targets can be worked on at home as well as in the nursery. The whole process may be difficult for some parents, and practitioners may have to rely on the good relationships they have built in order to support parents at this time. Some ideas on how to create and maintain good partnerships are presented on page 80.

Ideas to try

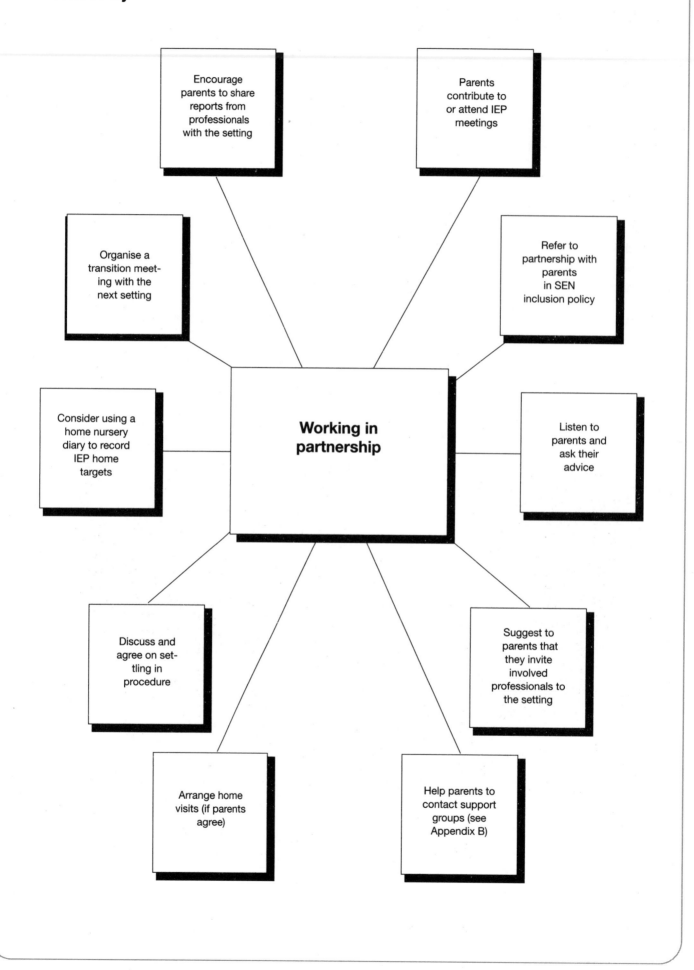

Encourage parents to share reports from professionals with the setting

Parents contribute to or attend IEP meetings

Organise a transition meeting with the next setting

Refer to partnership with parents in SEN inclusion policy

Consider using a home nursery diary to record IEP home targets

Working in partnership

Listen to parents and ask their advice

Discuss and agree on settling in procedure

Suggest to parents that they invite involved professionals to the setting

Arrange home visits (if parents agree)

Help parents to contact support groups (see Appendix B)

STEP 5

After an agreed period, usually a term or three months, a **review meeting** is held. This is an integral part of the IEP process. The key worker, Pre-school setting SENCO and parents should all attend and the child's progress towards the targets is discussed.

The review meeting is also an opportunity for both setting and parents to update information and pass on any new developments. Practitioners may find it helpful to do some observations of the child before the meeting so they have the latest report on the child's progress.

It should be a positive meeting and one which celebrates what the child has achieved.

Each IEP target should be looked at in turn and an evaluation made as to whether or not the child has reached the target. It is helpful to note any particular strategies or resources that have been successful and those which have not really worked. In this way a picture emerges of how best to support a child which in turn forms a useful record for future planning.

Where a child does not achieve his/her targets it is always worth considering if they were realistic and achievable within the time frame (**SMART**) before deciding on revised or new targets.

(See 'Individual Education Plan', pages 83 and 84.)

There are three basic outcomes to an IEP review meeting.

1. The child makes progress towards the targets but continues to need support to do so. Another IEP is written at 'Early Years Action' and new targets are set.

2. The child makes considerable progress and may even surpass the targets. It is judged by the meeting that extra support is **no longer needed** to maintain this progress. No further IEP is written but the child continues to be monitored.

3. The child has not made adequate progress towards the targets or is falling further behind peers. **Additional advice or assessment** is needed from outside support agencies/specialist teachers or health professionals. With additional advice, an IEP is written at 'Early Years Action Plus'.

   Apart from exceptional circumstances, this is usually only an option after two or three IEP cycles.

Early Years Action Plus

Children at Early Years Action Plus are subject to the same IEP planning and review cycle as those at Early Years Action. The main difference is that there are often more professionals involved. These may include speech and language therapists, physiotherapists, etc.

These professionals should be invited to IEP meetings and asked for reports and suggestions for targets for the child. A note should be made on the Individual Education Plan of any contributions made by a professional to show that you as a setting are listening to specialist advice.

Keeping track of all those who need to be invited can be quite a task so it is useful to keep a record for your own benefit.

(See Appendix A. Annual Record of Children with Special/Additional needs and IEP/Review meeting checklist).

Statutory Assessment

There are a small minority of children whose needs are deemed to be severe, complex and life-long. These children may well need to go through the 'Statutory Assessment' procedure or request such an assessment. There are clear guidelines in the Code of Practice about how this is to be carried out and local authorities have to meet various standards and timescales. They also have a duty to provide support for parents through Parent Partnership Groups. Information and advice on this process should be sought through local agencies.

Hands-on activity

You would like a child *to be able to sit for a short time and participate within a small group.*

Use the example above to help you to write an IEP target.

Individual Education Plan

INDIVIDUAL EDUCATION PLAN No. .... EYA / EYA+ / ST

Child's name: D.O.B.

Targets set Date:	Review Date:
Target 1 Action/Strategies/Resources By whom	Achieved? What has/has not been successful?
Target 2 Action/Strategies/Resources By whom	Achieved? What has/has not been successful?
Target 3 Action/Strategies/Resources By whom	Achieved? What has/has not been successful?

IEP Review Contd

Child's strengths:

Parent/Child's comments:

Additional/New information:

New IEP needed?   Yes/No   Change in Code of Practice?   Yes/No

Further steps/Action:

Those involved in writing/reviewing IEP (Including reports/advice) or needing copies:

New IEP written   Yes/No

Date of next IEP review:

Name of person completing this form:

Position:

Child participation

It is always important to consider the views of a child when planning and reviewing, not only Individual Education Plans and targets, but also methods of support. With very young children or those who have limited communication skills this can be a challenge.

▶ Children will often find it easier to express themselves through drawing and this can be a way forward in trying to collect together their thoughts and feelings onto paper.

▶ Carefully managed 'conferencing' is another way of a familiar adult talking to children to find out what they are thinking and how they are feeling. By asking the right sort of questions staff can give children an opportunity to express what they like, what they find difficult, how they like to play or learn.

▶ More general questioning can provide a profile of a child's likes, dislikes, friends, special people, favourite activities and what makes them upset or happy. Where a child has an IEP it can be helpful to focus the questions around the targets.

Let's look back at one suggested target for an Individual Education Plan earlier in the chapter.

▶ to play a turn-taking game

▶ with one other child and the key worker

▶ for 10 minutes each day

▶ using the shopping and bus stop games

▶ with one person taking the turn wearing a hat

Focused questions you could ask when conferencing with a child include:

▶ What do you like doing at nursery?

▶ What don't you like doing?

▶ What games do you like?

▶ What is your favourite game?

▶ What do you think you are good at?

▶ Who do you play with?

▶ Who are the grown-ups who help you?

Practitioners can record the child's answers onto a record sheet which can contribute to a review (see 'My targets' and 'I like . . . sheets on pages 87 and 88).

An alternative is to tape or video the conversation. This can be a very powerful tool. It is always best to check with parents first if you are going to use this method of recording.

Golden rules for child participation

▶ Choose your moment carefully. The child needs to be settled and happy.

▶ Time your conversation to coincide with the target activity, e.g. either just before or just after you have played the game.

▶ Make sure that you are in a slightly quieter area of your setting so you can talk without interruption.

▶ Put your conversation into context for the child, e.g. 'You know we play our special game together? Well I thought we could chat about how we are getting on'.

▶ If you are going to write anything down, explain why – e.g. 'I'm going to write down what you say so that I can tell your mum about it'.

▶ Ask *open* questions to give the child an opportunity to express themself.

▶ Encourage the child to contribute with drawing or mark making. Simple frames can support this.

▶ Accept what a child says without any comment, apart from encouraging them to continue or to clarify what they mean.

▶ Stop if the child is uncomfortable or does not want to talk. You can always try at another time.

My targets

by ....

Date: ....

 **My name is**

I like

I can

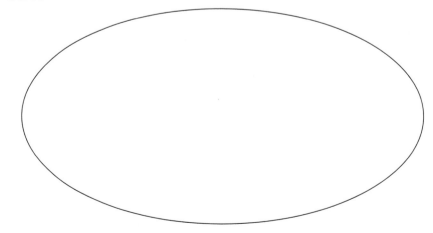

Date: ....

Support, advice and assistance: people you may meet

There is an increasing move towards a more seamless and coherent support for children with special needs and their families. There is recognition of the need to bring both health and education services together and create co-ordinated provision. Within both health and education services there are, however, various professionals that you may encounter.

Remember: parental permission must be obtained before any discussion with a professional outside your Pre-school.

Local authorities and Early Years Development and Childcare Partnerships have a range of services to support Pre-school settings. These may include:

▶ *Curriculum advisers*

These are teachers who can give advice and support on curriculum and planning issues. They will advise on general good practice throughout the Pre-school.

▶ *Inclusion adviser/area SENCO*

These are teachers or early years specialists who can advise on inclusion and working with children with special needs. They often have extensive experience or specialist qualifications in working with children with particular needs, such as hearing or visual impairments. Some are involved in direct teaching while others fulfil a more advisory role.

▶ *Portage worker*

Portage is a home teaching service. It works with children who have special needs aged 0–5 years and their families. Portage workers visit children in their homes on a regular basis to assess and teach new skills. They model the teaching of each skill to enable parents and carers to work with their child in between visits. In this way parents and workers are able to work together, pool their knowledge of the child and support each other. Many authorities have portage workers or those who carry out a similar role.

▶ *Educational psychologist*

Educational psychologists provide specialist assessment of all kinds of learning difficulties. They can give advice on teaching and management strategies and behaviour management. They will always become involved if a child is having a Statutory Assessment.

▶ *The Pre-school Learning Alliance*

While this organisation is not run by local authorities it often works closely with EYDCPs. The workers are experienced practitioners with a wide range of knowledge and expertise who can help, support and advise on a variety of issues.

Local health service professionals include:

▶ *Clinical psychologist*

Clinical psychologists work within health service settings. They provide individual and family counselling, family therapy and advice. They can advise and support on a variety of issues including behaviour management and conditions such as autism.

▶ *Speech and language therapist*

Speech and language therapists will assess, give advice to families and work directly with children who have a speech, language or communication disorder.

They also work with children who have related eating and swallowing difficulties, giving advice on feeding, sucking, food, and mouth and tongue movement.

▶ *Physiotherapist*

Physiotherapists work mainly with children with physical difficulties or delay. They give advice and support and plan individual programmes which centre on issues such as exercise, co-ordination and balance. They will also advise on specialist equipment like splints, braces, wheelchairs and buggies.

▶ *Occupational therapist*

Occupational therapists work with children who need help in developing practical life skills because of some form of physical, psychological or social delay or disability. They provide advice and access to specialised equipment both at home and in the Pre-school, such as chairs, bathing or toileting aids and adaptations to everyday items.

▶ *Community doctors and paediatricians*

Doctors and paediatricians work alongside parents to identify and diagnose various illnesses or conditions. They monitor medical conditions as the child grows older and can also refer to other health service professionals.

▶ *Health visitors*

Every Pre-school child has a health visitor allocated through their local GP. Health visitors will visit families at home when a child is born and also run various clinics for immunisations, sleep and general development checks. They are available for help, support and advice on all development and health issues.

▶ *Social workers*

Social workers support children and families in difficult circumstances. They can provide advice and access to other social services provision such as respite care. They will also become involved when there are child protection issues or procedures in place.

Things to consider

Do you know how to contact a range of professionals?

Do you know where they are based?

Is there a local directory of children's services?

Are you aware of local voluntary organisations and charities?

Have you established links with community groups?

Hands-on activity

▶ Begin to compile your own list of local services and contacts.

▶ Contact one of the national organisations or charities to find out more about their work. Share this information with your colleagues or fellow students.

The contacts listed in Appendix B may be a good starting point.

A case study to illustrate the use of the proformas presented in this chapter

Observation Sheet

Child's name: *Lucy Bloggs* **Date:** *08.01.06*

Focus of observation: *Physical development*

<u>Time</u>	
10 a.m.	*Start observation*
	Lucy happy to tackle course, lined up with friends but was looking to Mary (key worker) for support.
	Held Mary's hand and climbed up first step, was encouraged to climb next one herself - managed to do this.
	Say's 'I can't' and sits down on step. Supported by Mary and with a great deal of help manages two more steps. Hand in hand.
	Lucy then comes down the short slide. Gets her leg caught under her and shouts for Mary to help her. Mary pulls Lucy's leg from under her and holds her hand as she comes down slide. Lucy sits at the bottom of the slide and calls for Mary to help her get off. Mary helps her.
	Lucy goes over to a small barrel on stand. Encouraged by Mary to kneel down and crawl through. Lucy does this with a fair amount of effort. Mary encourages but does not touch Lucy. Lucy gets through 'you are clever' says Mary. Lucy grins and says 'again'.
	Repeats the activity 3 more times and is praised by Mary each time. Lucy says 'I tired' and goes inside for a drink.
10.20	*Observation over*

Observation Follow-up

What was noticed

Lucy was happy to engage in the activity.
Lucy managed some of the steps herself.
Lucy needed lots of support from Mary (key worker).
Lucy was prepared to try to go higher with support on the steps.
Lucy got her leg caught under her at the top of the slide.
Lucy called for Mary's support before she tried herself.
Lucy could crawl through the barrel unaided.
Lucy enjoyed the barrel activity as she did it three more times.

What this could tell us

Lucy is willing to try but lacks confidence.
Lucy seems to call for help before trying herself.
Lucy seems to find some of the activities hard.
Lucy seems more comfortable with ground-level activities, e.g. the barrel.
Lucy responds well to praise and encouragement.

What we should do next

Ask Mrs Bloggs how Lucy's physical development is at home.
Meet with Lucy's mother to discuss an IEP.
Possible targets to include regular practice on outdoor equipment at home/school.
Ask Mary (key worker) to encourage Lucy without offering help too quickly.

Observed by: Kia Jones   **Discussed with:** Mary Smith

Parental Meeting Sheet

Record of meeting with parent(s)   **Date:** *15th January 06*

Child's name: *Lucy Bloggs*   **D.O.B.** *25.12.02*

Present at meeting: *Mrs Bloggs (mother), Mary Smith (key worker), Kia Jones (SENCO)*

Reason for the meeting:
The setting staff are concerned about Lucy's physical development. She does not seem to like outdoor play and struggles with the equipment, needing her key worker's one-on-one support.

Information/What was discussed:
Mary set out her concerns to Mrs Bloggs. Kia shared with Mrs Bloggs the observations that staff had carried out. The staff stressed that Lucy was very happy within the setting and was always prepared to try new things, even during outside play.

Mrs Bloggs reported that Lucy had broken her leg when she was very small; since then Mrs Bloggs has been very protective of her.

Mrs Bloggs informed staff that she and Lucy lived in a high-rise flat with no stairs or garden. Mrs Bloggs said she did not take Lucy to the park as she is worried she may hurt herself while playing. When she takes Lucy out she makes sure she holds her hand at all times as she wants to ensure Lucy's safety.

What should happen next:
- *Mrs Bloggs will be invited to see the children at play in the pre-school garden so she can see the high level of supervision the children have.*

- *An IEP will be set up to teach Lucy new skills and build on those skills she is struggling with at this moment in time.*

- *The IEP will have home and school targets*

Signed: *Kia Jones*   **(setting)**   **Signed:** *M. Bloggs*   **(parent)**

Individual Education Plan

INDIVIDUAL EDUCATION PLAN No. .1.........	EYA / EYA+ / ST

Child's name: *Lucy Bloggs*   D.O.B. *25.12.02*

Targets set **Date:** *30.1.06*	**Review** **Date:** *2.5.06*
Target 1	Achieved?
Lucy will climb unaided up the five steps to the top of the slide.	What has/has not been successful?
Action/Strategies/Resources	
Lucy will be taken outside for group activities twice a day. Initially Lucy will be offered physical support gradually reducing to verbal support and praise.	
By whom	
All nursery staff. Overseen by Mary (key worker).	
Target 2	
Lucy will come down the slide at school and at the park by herself.	Achieved? What has/has not been successful?
Action/Strategies/Resources	
Lucy will be supported to use the slide daily at Pre-school and as often as possible by her mum at the park.	
By whom	
All staff. Mary (Key worker will arrange when and by whom). Mrs Bloggs.	

IEP Review Contd.

Target 3

Lucy will be confident enough to self select outdoor play.

Achieved?
What has/has not been successful?

Action/Strategies/Resources

Lucy will be taken to play outside and encouraged to try new equipment. Staff will plan outdoor games with groups to include Lucy.

By whom

All staff. Mary (key worker will arrange when and by whom).

Hands-on activities

Complete the support cycle by writing a review of Lucy's IEP.

Consider if she would need another IEP and if so what targets would you set next.

Remember to include Mrs Bloggs's views and comments.

Imran attends your Pre-school. He is three years old and has been at the setting for a month. He seems settled and happy. His key worker is concerned about his language development and reports that 'she can't understand what he is saying'.

If you were the SENCO, what action would you take?

The Code of Practice describes 'special educational needs' as falling into four categories. Referring back to this chapter remind yourself what these are:

1.

2.

3.

4.

If a child has a difficulty with speaking and language, which category would he/she be in?

If a child found it difficult to walk, which category would he/she be in?

Themed observations (see Step 2 of 'A graduated response')

What kind of activity might you set up to gain information about a child's physical abilities?

What kind of activity might you set up to gain information about a child's language abilities?

 Further reading

Department for Education and Employment (DfEE) (2001) *Special Educational Needs Code of Practice*. London: DfEE.
Department for Education and Skills. DFES (2001) *The SEN Toolkit*. London: DFES.
Drifte, C. (2005) *A Manual for the Early Years SENCO*. London: Paul Chapman Publishing.

 Glossary

Augmentative Communication: This is any system of communication which supports and complements the spoken word, such as Makaton.

Disability Discrimination Act 1995 (DDA): Legislation which has applied to the provision of day care since 1996. The coverage of the DDA was extended by the Special Educational Needs and Disability Act of 2001, to include education and associated services. From September 2002 it has been unlawful to discriminate against disabled children in the provision of any services.

Early Years Action: Part of the 'graduated response' outlined in the Code of Practice. When a child is identified by a practitioner and SENCO as having additional needs which require interventions that are additional to or different from those usually provided these are recorded in an Individual Education Plan.

Early Years Action Plus: Part of the graduated response outlined in the Code of Practice. When a child is identified as having a special educational need and advice and/or support is provided by outside specialists or professionals. Interventions which are additional to or different from the strategies provided at Early Years Action are put into place. An Individual Education Plan is written.

Early Years Foundation Stage (EYFS): The proposed title of the early years curriculum which combines the Birth to Three Matters guidance and the Foundation Stage Curriculum.

Foundation Stage: The Foundation Stage begins when a child reaches three and lasts until the end of the school Reception year. There is a Foundation Stage Curriculum which pre-schools follow encompassing six areas of learning.

Graduated Response: A model of action and intervention designed to help children with special educational needs. It recognises that there is a continuum of needs which sometimes calls for increasing levels of specialist advice and support.

Individual Education Plan (IEP): This is a plan of action designed to meet the additional needs of individual children. It contains targets and strategies to help children meet those targets. It is a working document that is usually reviewed each term.

Makaton: A system of signs and symbols used to support those with speech and language difficulties.

Ofsted: The Office for Standards in Education is a government department. It takes responsibility for inspecting and reporting on the standards and performance of all educational settings.

Special Educational Needs Co-ordinator (SENCO): The person responsible for the day-to-day operation of a setting's special needs policy and procedures.

 APPENDIX A

Sample Admissions Policy

Annual record of children with special or additional needs

Weekly record of progress towards targets

IEP/Review meeting checklist

Sample Admissions Policy

Statement of intent

It is our intention here at …………................…………… to make our Pre-school genuinely accessible to children and families from all sections of the local community. In order to support this ethos we:

▶ Treat individuals in a fair and inclusive way regardless of any additional need, gender, background, religion, ethnicity or competency in spoken English. We make our equal opportunity policy widely known.

▶ Ensure the existence of our Pre-school is widely known in the local community. We will place notices advertising the group widely.

▶ Welcome applications from families with children with special needs and always attempt to provide an appropriate level of care and consult widely with outside agencies in regard of training and support.

▶ Try to be flexible about attendance patterns so as to accommodate the needs of individual families, parents/carers and childminders.

The basis of our admissions policy at ………………….................…………… is our official registration with the Office for Standards in Education (**Ofsted**), which sets out the number and ages for which places can be provided.

We never exceed the adult-to-children ratios that are set out in our registration:

(set out individual details of numbers of places in your setting and how to apply below)

This policy has due regard for all children who attend our setting.
This policy links to our other setting policies, specifically:

▶ Equal Opportunities Policy

▶ Inclusion Policy

▶ Working with Parents and Carers Policy

▶ Settling-in Policy and procedures

This policy was written with reference to the **National Day Care Standards** (Ofsted's *Sessional Day Care: Guidance to the National Standards*).

Annual record of children with special or additional needs

Child's name	D.O.B.	Date of admission	EYA/EYA+/STAT	Date of first IEP	Review date	Outcome	Review date	Outcome

Abbreviations: EYA: Early Years Action   EYA+: Early Years Action Plus   STAT: Statemented

IEP: Individual Education Plan   Outcome: Does the child remain at the same stage?

Weekly record of progress towards targets

Child's name		Key worker		
Date	Progress towards IEP target			
IEP target				

IEP/Review meeting checklist

Child's name   Date of IEP/review meeting

Person or professional	Name	Invited Yes/No	Reply report	Sent

IEP/Review meeting checklist

APPENDIX B

Contacts,
training and resources

Curriculum guidance and advice

England
Sure Start
Email: birth-to-3-matters.mailbox@dfes.gsi.gov.uk
www.surestart.gov.uk

The Early Childhood Unit
www.earlychildhood.org.uk

QCA (Qualifications and Curriculum Authority)
Curriculum Guidance for the Foundation Stage
Sets of materials on diversity and inclusion
www.qca.org.uk

Northern Ireland
Pre-school guidance
www.deni.gov.uk/preschool

Children's services: Northern Ireland
www.childrensservicesnorthernireland.com

Scotland
Scottish Qualifications Authority
www.sqa.org.uk

Children in Scotland
www.childreninscotland.org.uk

Learning and Teaching Scotland
www.ltscotland.org.uk

Wales
Qualifications Curriculum and Assessment Authority for Wales
www.accac.org.uk

Children in Wales
www.childreninwales.org.uk

Further reading

Department for Education and Skills (DfES) (2001) *Special Educational Needs Code of Practice*. Nottingham: DfES Publications.

Disability Rights Commission (2001) *SEN Disability Discrimination Act*. London: DRC.

Disability Rights Commission (2002) *DDA Code of Practice: Rights of Access to Goods, Facilities, Services and Premises*. London: DRC.

National Children's Bureau (2003) *Early Years and the Disability Discrimination Act 1995: What Service Providers Need to Know*. London: NCB.

Pre-school Learning Alliance (2004) *Working Towards a Better Practice: Special Educational Needs and Impairments*. London: Pre-school Learning Alliance.

Also see end-of-chapter references

Contacts

Chris Dukes and Maggie Smith (authors of the Hands on Guides)
www.hands-on-guides.co.uk

Action for Leisure
Tel: 020 8783 0173
Email: enquiries@actionforleisure.org.uk
Provides information, advice, training and publications

Afasic
50–52 Great Sutton Street
London EC1V 0DJ
Tel: 020 7490 9410 (administration)
Tel: 0845 355 5577 (helpline)
www.afasic.org.uk

Alliance for Inclusive Education
Unit 2, 70 South Lambeth Road
London SW8 1RL
Tel: 020 7735 5277
www.allfie.org.uk

British Council of Disabled People
Litchurch Plaza
Litchurch Lane
Derby DE24 8AA
Tel: 01332 295551
www.bcodp.org.uk

British Diabetic Association UK
10 Parkway
Camden
London NW1 7AA
Tel: 020 7424 1000
www.diabetes.org.uk

Brittle Bone Society
30 Guthrie Street
Dundee DD1 5BS
Tel: 01382 204446
www.brittlebone.org.uk

Centre for Accessible Environments
Nutmeg House
60 Gainford Street
London SE1 2NY
Tel: 020 7357 8182
www.cae.org.uk

Children in Scotland
5 Shandwick Place
Edinburgh EH3 4RG
Tel: 0131 228 8484
www.childreninscotland.org.uk

Disabled Living Foundation
Tel: 020 7829 6111
The DFL offers a free advice service on specialist equipment to people with impairments and their carers

Down's Syndrome Association
155 Mitcham Road
London SW17 9PG
Tel: 020 8682 4001
www.downs-syndrome.org.uk

Dyspraxia Foundation
8 West Alley
Hitchin
Hertfordshire SG5 1EG
Tel: 01462 454986
www.dyspraxiafoundation.org.uk

Epilepsy Action
Tel: 0113 210 8800
www.epilepsy.org.uk

Mencap
117–123 Golden Lane
London EC1Y 0RT
Tel: 020 7454 0454
www.mencap.org.uk

Muscular Dystrophy Campaign
Tel: 020 7720 8055
www.muscular-dystrophy.org.uk

National Association of Toy and Leisure Libraries
Tel: 020 7387 9592
Email: admin@natl.ukf.net

National Autistic Society
393 City Road
London EC1V 1NG
Tel: 020 7833 299
www.nas.org.uk

National Deaf Children's Society
Tel: 0808 800 8880
www.ndcs.org.uk
Information, training and advice

National Early Years Network
77 Holloway Road
London N7 8JZ
Tel: 020 7607 9573

Parents for Inclusion
Unit 2
70 South Lambeth Rd
London SW8 1RL
Tel: 0208 7735 7735

Pre-school Learning Alliance
Tel: 0208 7833 0991 (National)
www.pre-school.org.uk

REACH

Tel: 0845 1306225

www.reach.org.uk

Advice and support for children with hand and arm deficiencies

Royal National Institute of the Blind (RNIB)

105 Judd Street

London WC1H 9NE

Tel: 020 7388 1266

www.rnib.org.uk

Advice, support and information for parents and carers the blind and partially sighted

Royal National Institute for Deaf People (RNID)

19–23 Featherstone Street

London EC1Y 8SL

Tel: 020 7296 8199

www.rnid.org.uk

Scope

6 Market Road

London N7 9PW

Tel: 0808 800 3333

www.scope.org.uk

Sickle Cell Society

54 Station Road

London NW10 4UA

Tel: 020 7272 7774

www.sicklecellsociety.org

Whizz-Kidz

Tel: 0208 7233 600

Email: info@whizz-kidz.org.uk

Whizz-Kidz is a national charity aimed at improving independence for children with mobility difficulties.

Resources

Toys, play equipment and furniture

Davies Sports (Sports equipment suitable for all children)

Tel: 0845 1204515

www.daviessports.co.uk

Edventure Playtime Games (Specialists in playground games)
Tel: 01323 501040
www.edventureplaytimegames.co.uk

Fledglings
Tel: 01799 530412
Email: fledglings@btinternet.com

Formative Fun (Equipment and information on toys and games to support children with a wide variety of needs)
Tel: 0845 8900609
www.formativefun.com

Fun Junction (Toys and equipment to look at before purchase)
Tel: 08700 423584
www.funjunctiononline.com

HELO (Childcare products – baby change/high-chairs and seats)
Tel: 01284 772400
www.hel-o.co.uk

James Leckey Designs
Tel: 0800 318265
www.leckey.com

Jenx
Tel: 0114 285 3376
www.jenx.com

Happy Puzzle Company (Purpose-built puzzles and games especially good for children with dyspraxia)
Tel: 0870 873 8989

Rifton
Tel: 0800 387 475
www.rifton.com

Rompa Educational (Supplies sensory resources)
Tel: 0800 056 2323
www.rompa.com

Spacekraft
Tel: 01274 581007
Email: enquiries@spacekraft.co.uk

Step by Step (Resources to encourage physical development)
Tel: 01430 410515
www.tocki.co.uk

TFH
Tel: 01299 827820 (Special needs toys)
www.tfkuk.com

TOCKi (Specialist toys and equipment to suit a wide range of special needs)
Tel: 01430 410515
www.tocki.co.uk

Index